A GUIDE TO

# SURFRIDING
IN
# NEW ZEALAND

## WAYNE WARWICK

4TH REVISED EDITION

VIKING SEVENSEAS NZ LTD;
P.O. BOX 152, PARAPARAUMU,
NEW ZEALAND

## Acknowledgements

Contributions are hereby acknowledged in this revised fourth edition of the following individuals and institutions: NIWA (National Institute Of Water & Atmosphere Research Ltd.), in particular Dr. Andrew Laing. Meteorological Service Of NZ Ltd. Department Of Survey And Land Information. David Robinson of Ocean Fun Unlimited. South Island photographer Warren Hawke — all photographs in this edition are his, except those as indicated as being by Mike Spence, John Milek and Warren Buckle.

# INDEX

Welcome to the fourth revised edition of New Zealand's original surfriding guide book, published since 1968. This edition provides maps and information on over 327 surfriding locations around New Zealand's North and South Island coastlines. Combined with the map showing the Coastal Meteorological phone numbers providing daily wave, wind and tidal forecasts over 23 separate coastal areas, this latest edition will assist surfers in making the right decisions on where to travel for the best waves throughout most of New Zealand.

*Surfer Graham Carse*

# INTRODUCING NEW ZEALAND

New Zealand is comprised of two main islands and has a population of just over three million people and seventy million sheep, all living in a land area similar to that of Great Britain. It is situated some 1,200 miles southeast of Australia in the South Pacific Ocean. The North Island has over 70% of the country's total population while the South Island has the larger land area and is predominantly cooler in temperature than the North Island. These lower temperatures help to provide some of the best snow skiing fields in the world. These are situated along the magnificent mountain range known as the Southern Alps. The Auckland region with approximately one million people, has New Zealand's largest population followed by Christchurch and the country's capital city, Wellington.

The majority of New Zealanders are of European descent with some 250,000 indigenous Maoris who are of Polynesian origin. English is the common language, however the Maori culture and its language is also taught and spoken throughout the country.

Polynesians are presumed to have first arrived in New Zealand or Aotearoa, "land of the long white cloud" around the year 900 AD. European immigrants mainly from Great Britain commenced arriving after Captain Cook's discovery of New Zealand in 1769.

Internationally, New Zealanders are often referred to as "Kiwis", which is in fact a rare native bird of the country. The Maori name for the new immigrants was "Pakeha", meaning without colour and is still used to this day.

The country is a member of the British Commonwealth and has a government and legal system similar to England. Its economy is based mainly on agriculture, horticulture, manufacturing and tourism.

The geography of the country is renowned for being some of the most beautiful and varied in the world, considering its relatively small land area. Its scenery ranges from beautiful green forests and pastures and clean uncrowded white sandy beaches to majestic snow covered mountains. The country has a volcanic history which is evident in imposing semi active volcanoes like Mount Ruapehu on the central North Island plateau and in the geo-thermal areas of the nearby Bay of Plenty. The latter area especially in and around the city of Rotorua is a popular place to rest tired bodies in hot mineral spa pools.

Scenic changes occur quickly throughout this uncrowded and compact country, inspiring many visitors to describe New Zealand as an ideal tourist destination. It is hoped that travelling surfers will discover not only good surf but also some of the scenic delights it has to offer.

*Spring surf session, Mount Taranaki (Mt. Egmont)*

Singapore

Indonesia

Bali

New Guinea

EQUATOR

*Gilbert I.*

P

*New Hebrides*

*New Caledonia*

AUSTRALIA

*Norfolk Is.*

NEW ZEALAND

42°S

# GENERAL INFORMATION

Hawaiian Is.

I F I C
C E A N

Tokelau Is.

Samoa Is.

If you plan on an extended stay in New Zealand and wish to find employment remember temporary visitors permits without specific authority make it illegal to work. Unless of course you are an Australian, as both countries have a reciprocal agreement that allows their citizens to live and work in either country without regulation.

Casual seasonal work may be found by the enthusiastic in places like fruit growing areas during the picking season. Other types of employment will depend on your particular qualifications and visitor status.

Medical facilities are plentiful and of a high standard throughout New Zealand. The Government subsidises the country's health system and services are therefore available either free of charge or at a reasonable cost depending on whether you seek government or private medical care.

New Zealand has a strong horticultural and agricultural economic base and travellers should be patient with officers of the New Zealand Customs and the Agricultural and Fisheries Departments at ports of entry into the country. Some foreign plant and animal diseases could have a serious effect on New Zealand's economy.

There is no need to take any special precautions regarding food and drink contamination other than normal common sense. New Zealand is free of any dangerous land animals, however some species of spiders are capable of painful and occasionally lethal bites but it rarely happens. Shark attacks are also very rare. The surf lifesaving movement is well established at most popular beaches during the summer season. New Zealand's coastal waters need only be given the normal respect oceans deserve the world over.

Major credit cards are accepted throughout New Zealand for most retail and service charges.

Eating out in New Zealand is generally a safe and an increasingly pleasurable experience. There are many low budget international food franchises now operating throughout the country. Fresh fruit and vegetable shops and health food shops are plentiful as are road side fruit vendors in New Zealand's horticultural areas. The humble hamburger or fish and chips can also be enjoyed in virtually every New Zealand town or city. Medium priced restaurants are plentiful and the range and quality of the food and service has improved markedly in recent years. This is partly due to meeting the demands of the increased tourist traffic in New Zealand. Tipping is not common practise in New Zealand except in cases of extraordinary service.

Surfing equipment is readily available throughout New Zealand with virtually every beach town having some type of surfshop. The better ones often have a surfboard factory out the back, stocking up to date equipment and providing a surfboard repair service.

New Zealand and Australian surfers regularly travel across the Tasman Sea dividing the two countries, so the latest ideas in design and performance are quickly exchanged.

New Zealand's climate could best be described as temperate, with its seasons being the reverse of those in the Northern Hemisphere. Because we are a small island nation our weather can change quickly as weather patterns move across the country.

North of Auckland is known locally as the Winterless North and enjoys a subtropical climate. Temperatures drop steadily as you move South. For the surfer, board shorts and a sleeveless wetsuit vest is adequate protection on the warmest days of summer. During spring and autumn a "spring suit" will suffice and in winter a full length wetsuit is advisable. Wetsuit, boots and even gloves are popular in the southern regions of the country. Being a temperate climate means you can expect short heavy rain showers in summer followed by warm

sunshine. This will often produce humid conditions. Long periods of fine weather are not uncommon particularly in eastern regions, sometimes producing drought conditions. Prevailing winds are from the West.

Weather forecasts are usually reliable and can be found along with tidal and swell information in all national and regional newspapers and also on radio and television broadcasts. Television weather forecasts can be particularly useful as they usually include satellite pictures giving a more balanced perspective particularly of swell-producing tropical cyclones and depressions. It is possible to utilise the services of the meteorological office who will provide coastal weather forecasts including swell size, wind direction and speed, tide times and the general weather outlook. This

chapter includes a map showing the 0900 phone numbers providing this service throught New Zealand.

Following is a selection of previously published New Zealand weather maps showing a variety of swell-producing tropical cyclones, lows and depressions around New Zealand's coastline. The lower the isometric number the more intense the depression, which usually means higher winds and bigger waves.

New Zealand lies perpendicular to the prevailing wester-lies of the 34° to 46° S latitude that the country spans, thus the west coast of New Zealand receives more consistent swells than the east coast. The east coast receives most of its surf from low cyclonic weather patterns, some of which are not visible on normal media weather maps as they occur far out in the South Pacific Ocean. Others are more dramatic tropical cyclones which travel down from the North.

Combining information on weather patterns and offshore wind direction along with the most suitable tide for any surfing location featured in this book should improve your chances of successfully locating good surfing and windsurfing conditions.

It is gratefully acknowledged that the material on pages 15-17 and page 20 is reproduced by courtesy of OCEAN FUN UNLIMITED. The author recommends their publication "Surf New Zealand Calendar" with its tide tables as being of assistance to all serious surfers and is available at most surf shops and many bookshops throughout New Zealand.

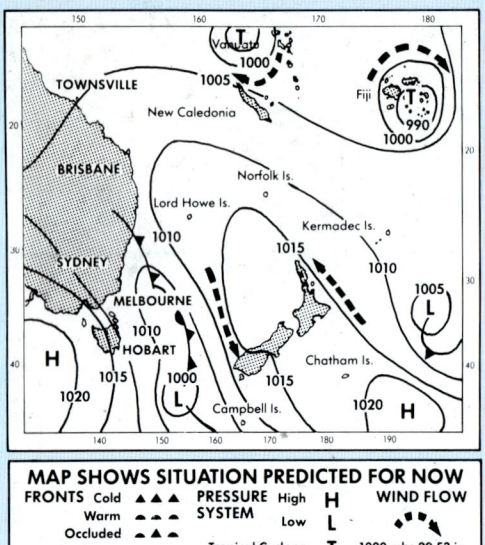

1. Swells from all directions!

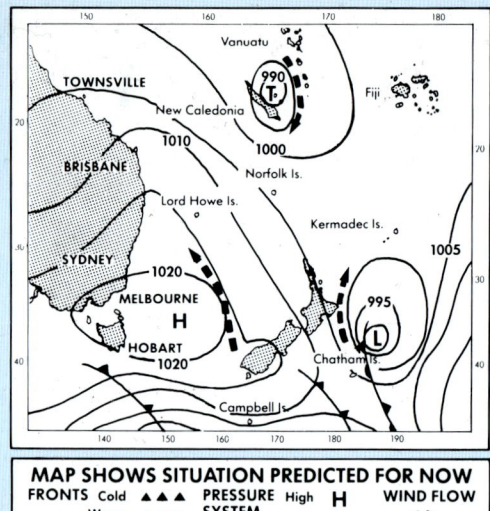

2. Swells from East Cape down to Cape Palliser and a tropical cyclone on the way.

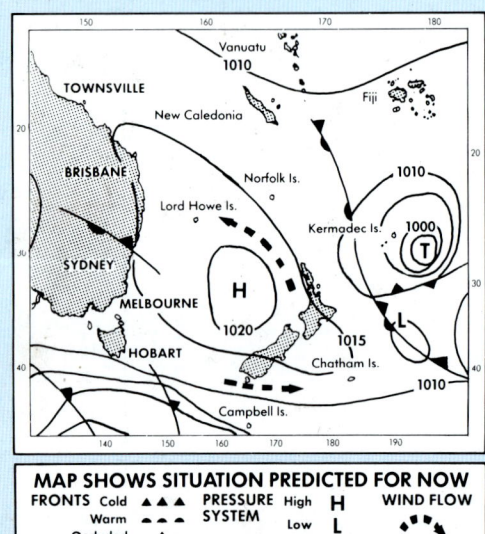

3. A tropical cyclone sending swells to the top half of the East Coast of the North Island.

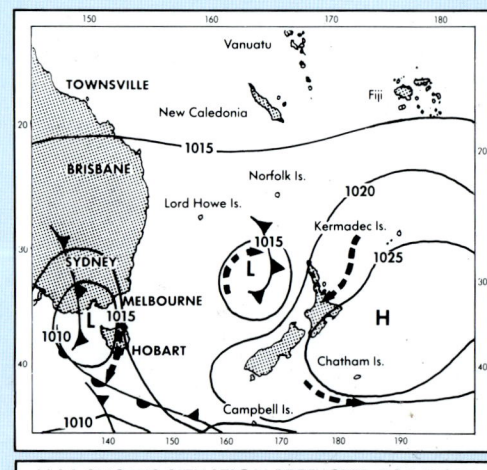

4. A low sending swells at the west coast of the North Island.

Springtime, Raglan. Photo John Milek

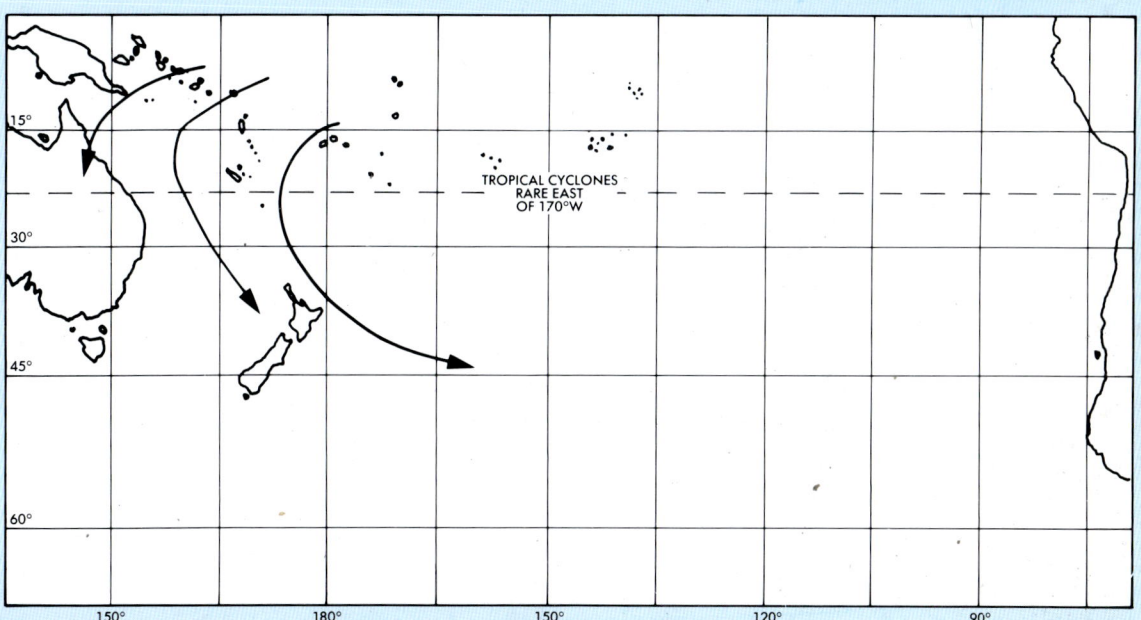

*Mangamanu, South Island. Photo Warren Hawke*

**TROPICAL CYCLONES RARE EAST OF 170°W**

**Common South Pacific Tropical Cyclone paths affecting New Zealand through the Summer Season December to March.**

*Taihoro Nukurangi*

©NIWA 1995

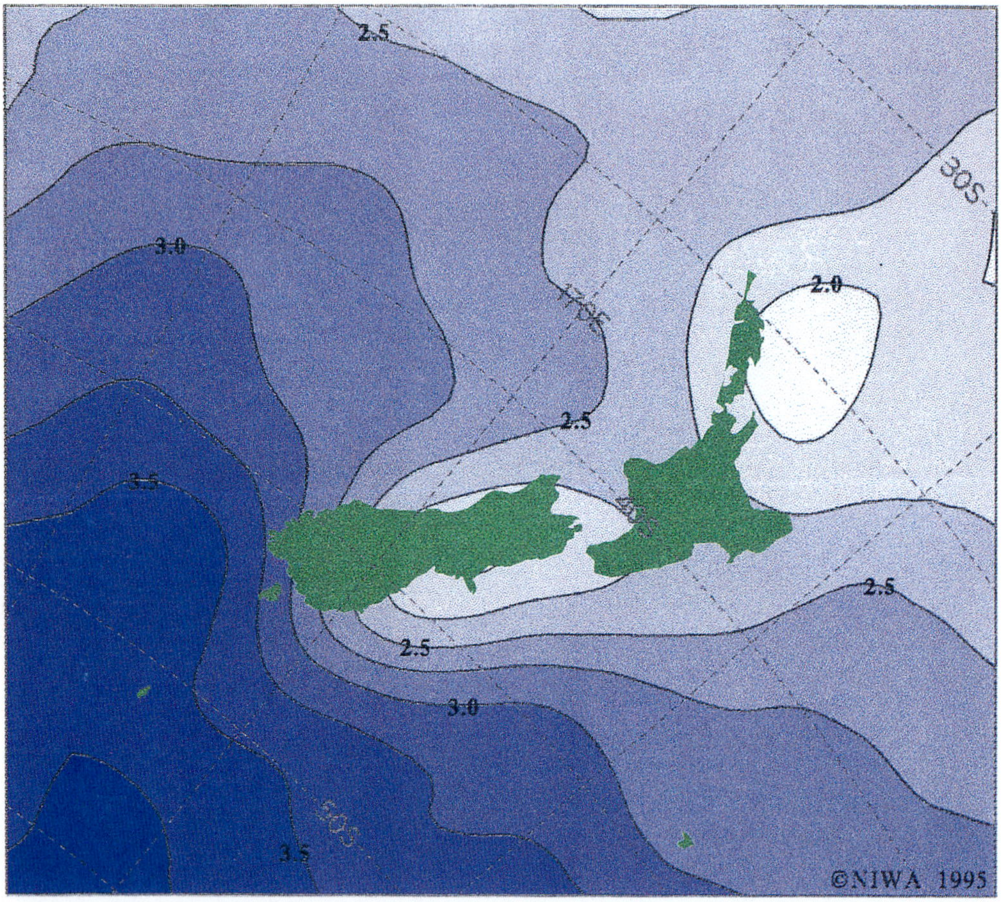

Mean significant wave height (in metres) derived from satellite data (Geosat). The coutours are at intervals of 0.25 m. The *significant wave height* is the average of the highest one-third of waves – this corresponds to a natural observation in which the most prominent waves tend to be noted. Some of the contours near to land may not be as accurate as those in open ocean. For example the satellite is unable to measure waves in Cook Strait and so these appear lower than they really are. The wave heights are a combination of both wind-sea and swell.

The "shadow" cast by the land is quite evident. the northeast of the North Island this is the result of the predominant west to southwest swells being blocked, and also to sheltering from the westerlies limiting local wind-sea growth. In other regions, whilst waves may be high for an onshore wind, limited wave growth in offshore winds reduces the overall average.

The average condition varies considerably from the 3.25 metres at the southwest tip of the country to less than 2.0 metres east of Northland.

*Reproduced by permission of NIWA.*

# TIME DIFFERENCE CONTOUR MAP

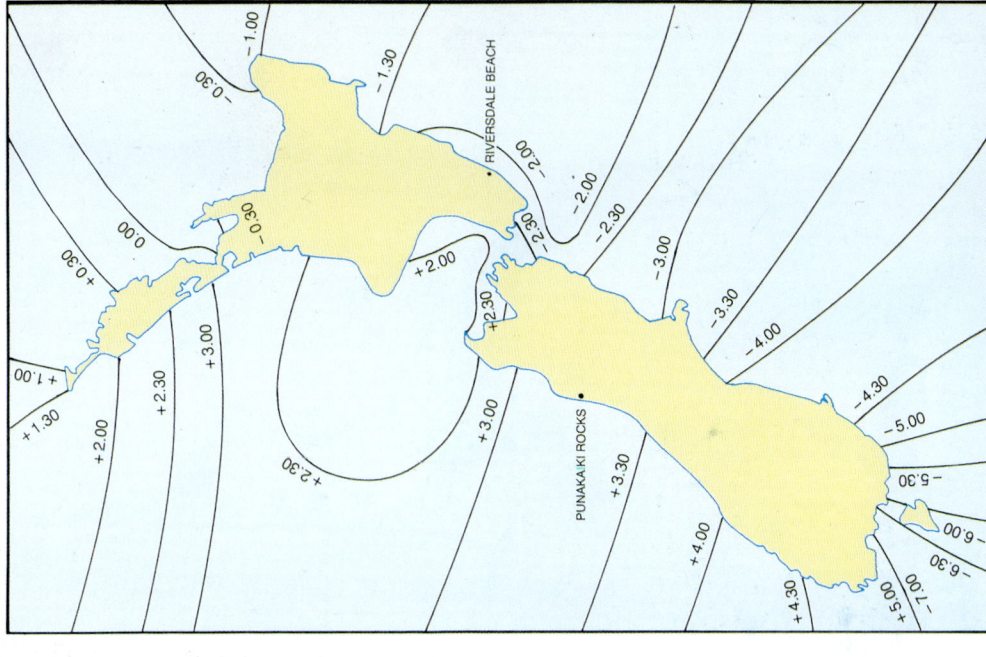

*Wainui Beach, Gisborne. Photo Mike Spence*

## USE THIS MAP TO FIND THE TIDE TIMES FOR ANY PLACE IN NEW ZEALAND

For example, to find the tide time difference for Riversdale Beach (see diagram, east coast, southern North Island), a time difference of minus 2 hours 15 minutes can be estimated. If a high tide occurs in Auckland (Waitemata) at 5.48 pm; subtracting 2hrs 15mn yields a high tide at 3.33 pm at Riversdale Beach.

Say you need to determine what the tide is doing at Punakaiki Rocks (see diagram West Coast, South Island) on a particular day at noon; and say the tide calendar shows that at Auckland (Waitemata) at noon, the tide is about halfway risen to the high tide. At Punakaiki, the diagram shows the tides **follow** (note the + time difference) Auckland by about 3 hours 15

minutes. With your pencil on the time calendar at noon, counting 3 hours 15 minutes **backwards** in time shows that at Punakaiki low tide is about noon. The time difference contour can be used to determine tide times anywhere in New Zealand. Predictions from the map will be most accurate on exposed eastern coasts near the Auckland area. Accuracy decreases with distance south; however, accuracy of one hour can still be expected for the deep south. Tide times in estuaries, river entrances, harbours and bays will almost always be later than indicated by the diagram due to time delays and water resistance caused by constricted flows.

# OCEAN CURRENTS

EAST CAPE CURRENT

EAST AUCKLAND CURRENT

TASMAN FRONT

CONTINENTAL SHELF

D'URVILLE CURRENT

WESTLAND CURRENT

SOUTHLAND CURRENT

TASMAN CURRENT

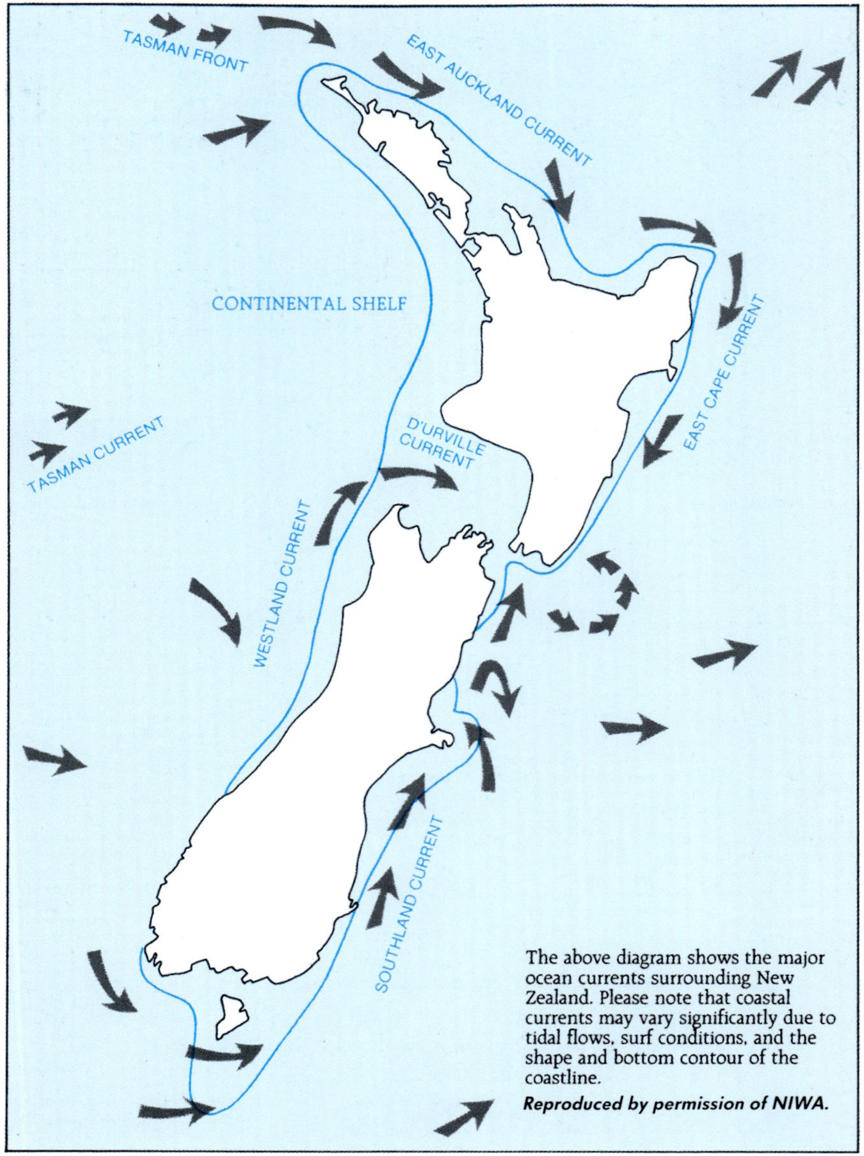

The above diagram shows the major ocean currents surrounding New Zealand. Please note that coastal currents may vary significantly due to tidal flows, surf conditions, and the shape and bottom contour of the coastline.

*Reproduced by permission of NIWA.*

# WIND DIRECTIONS

The diagram shows predominant wind directions over New Zealand. When taking winds of all speeds into consideration, wind that blows from a direction 20–35% of the time is shown with a ► Wind that blows from a direction more often, i.e. 36–55% of the time, is shown with a ►

For winds stronger than 16 knots, a ► indicates the wind blows from a direction 20–35% of the time, while a ► shows a more dominant wind which blows from a direction 36–55% of the time. In Christchurch, for example, the predominant wind is from the northeast. However, if the wind is strong, it is probably from the northeast or southwest. The winds reach Force 8 (34–40 knots) about 9 days a year, average wind speed is 8 knots, there are about 18 days of fog per year. 89 days of ground frost, 1974 hours of sunshine and 666ml of rain

Reproduced by permission of the NZ Meteorological Service

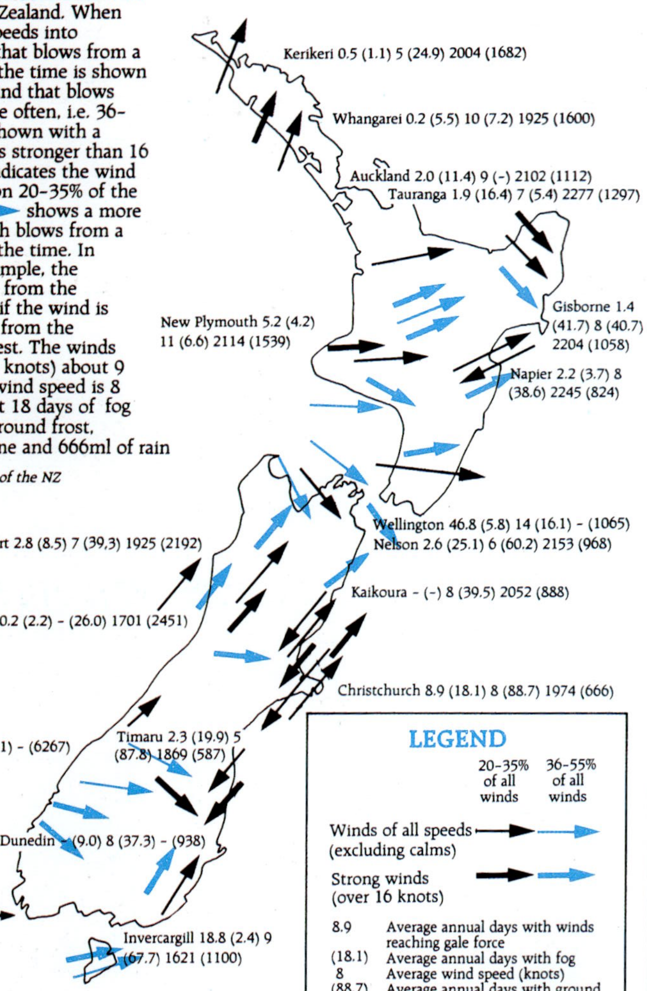

Kerikeri 0.5 (1.1) 5 (24.9) 2004 (1682)

Whangarei 0.2 (5.5) 10 (7.2) 1925 (1600)

Auckland 2.0 (11.4) 9 (–) 2102 (1112)

Tauranga 1.9 (16.4) 7 (5.4) 2277 (1297)

Gisborne 1.4 (41.7) 8 (40.7) 2204 (1058)

Napier 2.2 (3.7) 8 (38.6) 2245 (824)

New Plymouth 5.2 (4.2) 11 (6.6) 2114 (1599)

Wellington 46.8 (5.8) 14 (16.1) – (1065)

Nelson 2.6 (25.1) 6 (60.2) 2153 (968)

Kaikoura – (–) 8 (39.5) 2052 (888)

Christchurch 8.9 (18.1) 8 (88.7) 1974 (666)

Westport 2.8 (8.5) 7 (39.3) 1925 (2192)

Greymouth 0.2 (2.2) – (26.0) 1701 (2451)

Timaru 2.3 (19.9) 5 (87.8) 1869 (587)

Dunedin (9.0) 8 (37.3) – (938)

Invercargill 18.8 (2.4) 9 (67.7) 1621 (1100)

Milford Sound 5.7 (2.2) – (56.1) – (0267)

*Puysegur Point is the windiest known place in New Zealand*

## LEGEND

| | 20–35% of all winds | 36–55% of all winds |
|---|---|---|
| Winds of all speeds (excluding calms) | ► | ► |
| Strong winds (over 16 knots) | ► | ► |

8.9 Average annual days with winds reaching gale force
(18.1) Average annual days with fog
8 Average wind speed (knots)
(88.7) Average annual days with ground frost
1974 Average annual sunshine (hours)
(666) Average annual rainfall (ml)

# SEA AND AIR TEMPERATURES

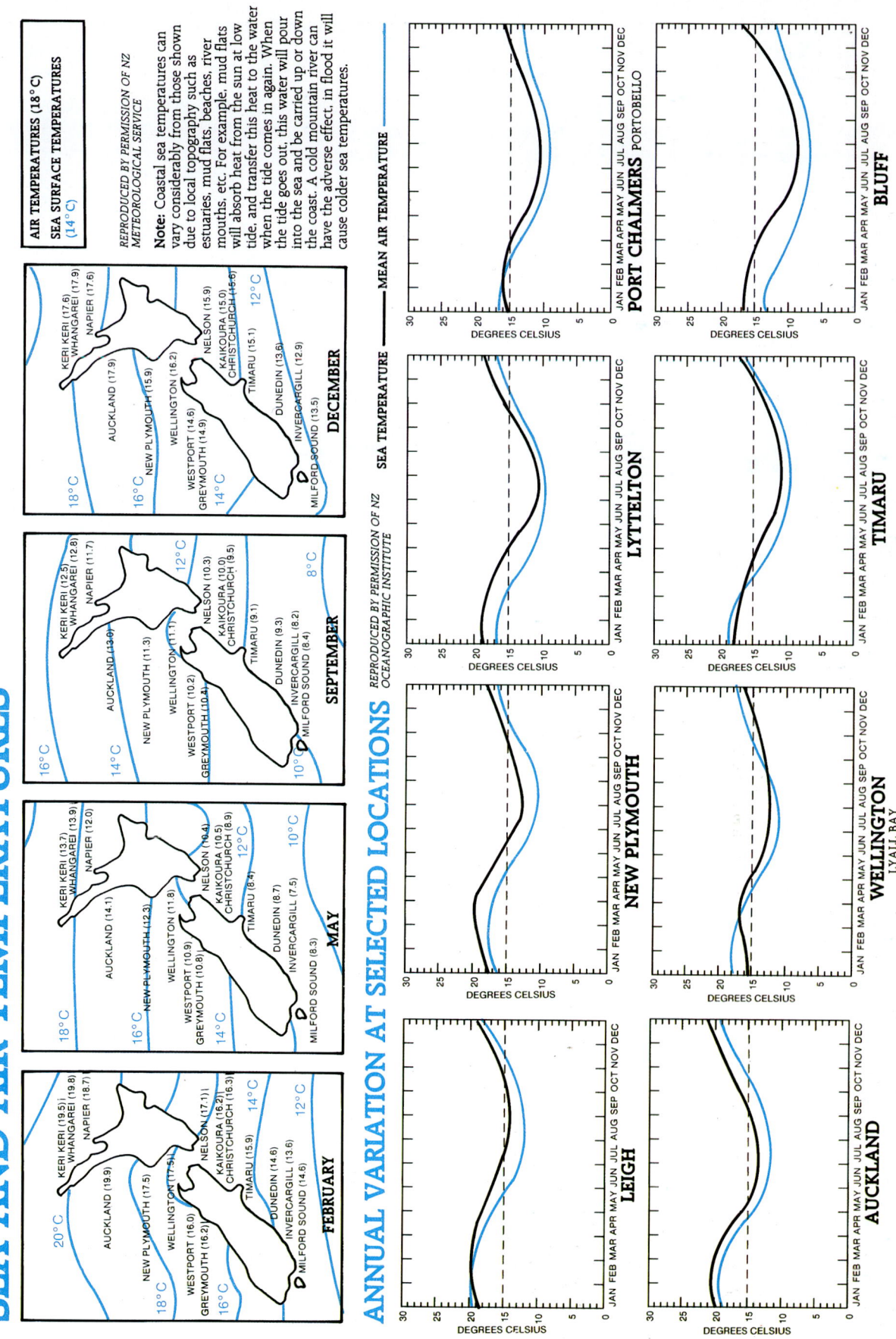

AIR TEMPERATURES (18°C)

SEA SURFACE TEMPERATURES (14°C)

*REPRODUCED BY PERMISSION OF NZ METEOROLOGICAL SERVICE*

**Note:** Coastal sea temperatures can vary considerably from those shown due to local topography such as estuaries, mud flats, beaches, river mouths, etc. For example, mud flats will absorb heat from the sun at low tide, and transfer this heat to the water when the tide comes in again. When the tide goes out, this water will pour into the sea and be carried up or down the coast. A cold mountain river can have the adverse effect, in flood it will cause colder sea temperatures.

**FEBRUARY**

KERI KERI (19.5) WHANGAREI (19.8)
NAPIER (18.7)
AUCKLAND (19.9)
NEW PLYMOUTH (17.5)
WELLINGTON (17.5)
WESTPORT (16.0)
GREYMOUTH (16.2)
NELSON (17.1)
KAIKOURA (16.2) CHRISTCHURCH (16.3)
TIMARU (15.9)
DUNEDIN (14.6)
INVERCARGILL (13.6)
MILFORD SOUND (14.6)
20°C 18°C 16°C 14°C 12°C

**MAY**

KERI KERI (13.7) WHANGAREI (13.9)
NAPIER (12.0)
AUCKLAND (14.1)
NEW PLYMOUTH (12.3)
WELLINGTON (10.9)
WESTPORT (10.8)
GREYMOUTH (10.8)
NELSON (10.4)
KAIKOURA (10.5) CHRISTCHURCH (8.9)
TIMARU (8.7)
DUNEDIN (8.7)
INVERCARGILL (7.5)
MILFORD SOUND (8.3)
18°C 16°C 14°C 12°C 10°C

**SEPTEMBER**

KERI KERI (12.5) WHANGAREI (12.8)
NAPIER (11.7)
AUCKLAND (13.0)
NEW PLYMOUTH (11.3)
WELLINGTON (11.1)
WESTPORT (10.2)
GREYMOUTH (10.4)
NELSON (10.3)
KAIKOURA (10.0) CHRISTCHURCH (9.5)
TIMARU (9.1)
DUNEDIN (9.3)
INVERCARGILL (8.2)
MILFORD SOUND (8.4)
16°C 14°C 12°C 10°C 8°C

**DECEMBER**

KERI KERI (17.6) WHANGAREI (17.9)
NAPIER (17.6)
AUCKLAND (17.9)
NEW PLYMOUTH (15.9)
WELLINGTON (16.2)
WESTPORT (14.6)
GREYMOUTH (14.9)
NELSON (15.9)
KAIKOURA (15.0) CHRISTCHURCH (15.6)
TIMARU (15.1)
DUNEDIN (13.6)
INVERCARGILL (12.9)
MILFORD SOUND (13.5)
18°C 16°C 14°C 12°C

# ANNUAL VARIATION AT SELECTED LOCATIONS

—— SEA TEMPERATURE ——   —— MEAN AIR TEMPERATURE ——

*REPRODUCED BY PERMISSION OF NZ OCEANOGRAPHIC INSTITUTE*

LEIGH

NEW PLYMOUTH

LYTTELTON

PORT CHALMERS PORTOBELLO

AUCKLAND

WELLINGTON LYALL BAY

TIMARU

BLUFF

DEGREES CELSIUS

JAN FEB MAR APR MAY JUN JUL AUG SEP OCT NOV DEC

17

# NEW ZEALAND MARINE WEATHER FORECAST AREAS

## MetPhone Coastal

**Coastal Weather Forecast Areas**
Named Areas limited by recognised coastal features

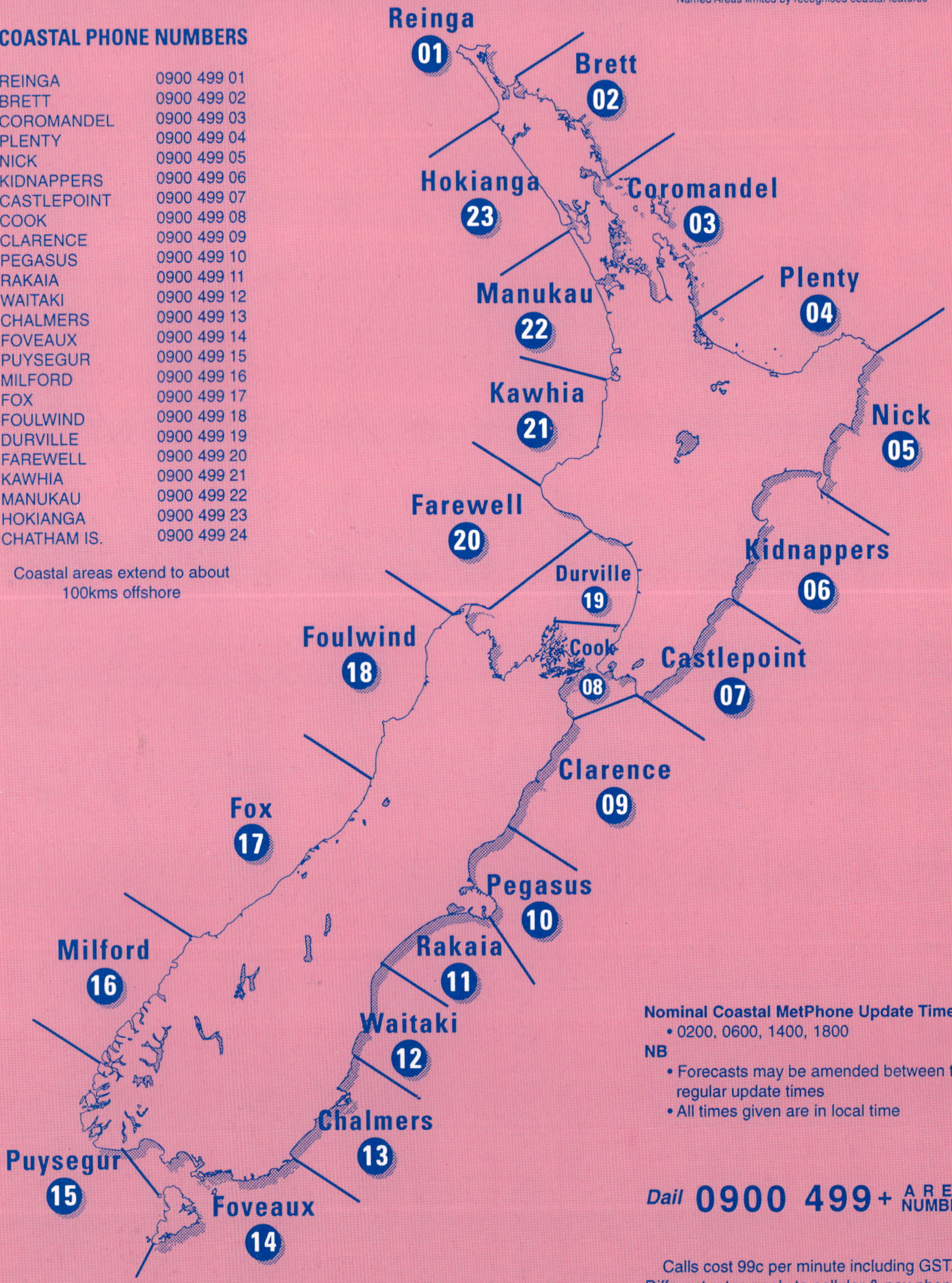

### COASTAL PHONE NUMBERS

| | |
|---|---|
| REINGA | 0900 499 01 |
| BRETT | 0900 499 02 |
| COROMANDEL | 0900 499 03 |
| PLENTY | 0900 499 04 |
| NICK | 0900 499 05 |
| KIDNAPPERS | 0900 499 06 |
| CASTLEPOINT | 0900 499 07 |
| COOK | 0900 499 08 |
| CLARENCE | 0900 499 09 |
| PEGASUS | 0900 499 10 |
| RAKAIA | 0900 499 11 |
| WAITAKI | 0900 499 12 |
| CHALMERS | 0900 499 13 |
| FOVEAUX | 0900 499 14 |
| PUYSEGUR | 0900 499 15 |
| MILFORD | 0900 499 16 |
| FOX | 0900 499 17 |
| FOULWIND | 0900 499 18 |
| DURVILLE | 0900 499 19 |
| FAREWELL | 0900 499 20 |
| KAWHIA | 0900 499 21 |
| MANUKAU | 0900 499 22 |
| HOKIANGA | 0900 499 23 |
| CHATHAM IS. | 0900 499 24 |

Coastal areas extend to about 100kms offshore

Reinga 01
Brett 02
Hokianga 23
Coromandel 03
Manukau 22
Plenty 04
Kawhia 21
Nick 05
Farewell 20
Kidnappers 06
Durville 19
Foulwind 18
Cook 08
Castlepoint 07
Clarence 09
Fox 17
Pegasus 10
Milford 16
Rakaia 11
Waitaki 12
Chalmers 13
Puysegur 15
Foveaux 14

**Nominal Coastal MetPhone Update Times**
• 0200, 0600, 1400, 1800
**NB**
• Forecasts may be amended between the regular update times
• All times given are in local time

*Dail* **0900 499 +** <sup>AREA NUMBER</sup>

Calls cost 99c per minute including GST.
Different rates apply to cellular & pay phones.

*Surfer Daniel Garbes*
*Photos by Warren Hawke*

# TRAVEL TIMES AND TIPS

The map shows most main road vehicle travel times. When searching for surf, watch the weather maps carefully, and use the MetPhone telephone services.

In general, the West Coast produces far more swell, bigger and more knarly, but it's also messier (aside from Raglan) and it has onshore (prevailing) winds. The swell rises and falls quickly. The East Coast waves are smaller but cleaner. It relies on ground swells and northeast blows. South of East Cape catches the consistent south swells. North of East Cape is inconsistent but superb; if there's waves, get there fast, as the swells only last a few days and then it's often flat again.

**Note On Travel Times**

Vehicle travel times are shown courtesy of the Automobile Association.

The times are based on a driver doing 80 km/hour on open stretches of road, plus a factor of five to ten minutes per hour for traffic delays. Be warned that speed cameras operate throughout New Zealand.

Most international travellers arrive in New Zealand on regular services via either Auckland, Wellington or Christchurch. Taxis and rental cars are available not only at most airports but also in towns and cities throughout the country. Camper vans are increasingly popular with tourists and are an excellent way to stay at remote surfing locations. A reasonably reliable second hand car can be purchased for about $2000.00 (NZ) upwards. New Zealand traffic drives on the left. Air New Zealand, Ansett Airlines, New Zealand Rail and the Intercity bus services are among those providing package tours worth investigation if you have limited time available.

These passenger services will carry surfboards but you must naturally ensure that they are adequately protected. Hitch-hiking is legal except on motorways and free-ways. It is a great way to meet the locals, but it can be time-consuming waiting for a ride, particularly if you are carrying a surfboard.

New Zealand's roading system is mainly of good quality and mostly tar sealed. Loose metal roads in remote areas are rapidly being upgraded.

Travellers should exercise caution driving on country roads as farmers often move large flocks of sheep or herds of cattle without advance warning.

Also remember to try and ask permission before crossing private land to reach remote surfing locations and leave all farm gates as you find them, closed or open. A little courtesy is usually well rewarded.

International drivers licences are recognised in New Zealand and should be obtained before your arrival if you plan on driving during your visit.

Accommodation is plentiful throughout the country except at some resort towns during the busy summer season from late December to late February. Hotels and motels are found almost everywhere and range from the cheap and humble to the luxurious and expensive. Most hotels are licensed to sell liquor, those that are not are known as private hotels. Unless you are a house guest, hotels — like liquor stores — cannot sell liquor to the public on Sundays. Some motels have licensed restaurants attached and others are self-contained with individual kitchen facilities.

The International Youth Hostel Association has cheap lodgings throughout New Zealand. Only members of the Association may stay at their hostels. If you are a foreigner, join the Association in your own country before departing. Be sure to travel with a sleeping bag when using Youth Hostels.

Motorcamps and camping grounds can be found almost everywhere throughout New Zealand and provide clean sleeping, washing and cooking facilities at reasonable prices. If you are not travelling with a campervan, caravan or tent, then camping grounds often have fully self-contained cabins for hire. The New Zealand Automobile Association produces excellent road maps and also guide books on the motels and camping grounds on New Zealand.

When travelling by road between the North and South Islands it would be wise to book ahead to reserve a space for your vehicle on one of the car ferries. They travel each day between Wellington in the North Island to Picton in the South Island. In settled weather you will enjoy some beautiful scenery.

A 'woodie' at New Plymouth. Photo C. Hewens

Early days at "The Wall," Lyall Bay, Wellington.

Waipu Cove 1963. Photo Warren Buckle

It is commonly believed that surfriding originated in the Hawaiian Islands and was practised almost exclusively by members of Hawaiian royal families, hence surfriding's now anachronistic title, "Sport of Kings."

When Captain Cook discovered Hawaii in 1778, surfriding was already an established sport, with members of royal families competing in races that took them out beyond the line of breakers and then catching a wave back in. The boards they competed on were up to sixteen feet in length and weighed over 50 kilograms. Many Hawaiians showed great interest in these surfriding contests and gambling on the results was quite common. Due to this gambling it was not surprising that in 1821 when the first missionaries arrived in the "Islands", surfriding was denounced as a corruptive pastime and a total ban was imposed on its practice. After 1900, when the strength of the church over the Hawaiian people began to weaken, surfriding was revived and has been enjoyed ever since.

Looking at surfriding as it is today in New Zealand with its own New Zealand Surfriders Association it is important to remember how closely it was once associated with the surf lifesaving movement.

Since lifesaving was practised in and around the sea, it was only natural that lifesavers were the first to try surfriding. Their inspiration for trying the sport came unquestionably from the late Duke Kahanamoku, once famous for his swimming feats in the Olympic Games. The Duke visited New Zealand and Australia in 1915 with George Cunha and gave a series of swimming and surfriding exhibitions. One of these exhibitions was at Lyall Bay, Wellington, in the North Island of New Zealand. One older member of the Maranui Surf Lifesaving Club in Wellington recalls the Duke's first ride at Lyall Bay, which was probably the first wave ever ridden in New Zealand. The Duke paddled out into the middle of the bay in quite a heavy swell, turned the board around and caught a wave and rode it until a short distance from the shore. He then ran to the front of the board so that it nosedived and he dived off into the wave and bodysurfed the rest of the way in. His ride created a lot of excitement among

the lifesavers present and it was not long after that, that they too were trying the sport. Thus began the great sport of surfriding in New Zealand.

In New Zealand during the 1920's surfers were using solid wooden sixteen foot boards styled on the Hawaiian models. One of these surfers was Edward Hughes of the Maranui Surf Lifesaving Club in Wellington. It is related by some of the older members of the club, that Mr Hughes competed and won first place in a Pacific Games Contest between Australia, New Zealand and Hawaii in the late 1920's. A decade was to pass after the introduction of solid wooden boards before a new style, the hollow Hawaiian paddle board was brought to New Zealand.

In the early 1940's surfskis designed in Australia were introduced and are sometimes still used for rescue work by the Lifesaving movement.

Around 1955 surfriding in Hawaii and California, was developing part of its present identity. Many of its enthusiasts no longer combined surf lifesaving with surfriding, they took to riding boards as a full

# THE EARLY YEARS OF SURFRIDING IN NEW ZEALAND

"Indicators," Raglan, West Coast, North Island, the first of the three main sections of New Zealand's most famous surfing location. First ridden by Peter Miller on February 28th, 1960, using a hollow 10 foot plywood surfboard. Photo John Milek

time sport. This attitude toward surfriding, first had an effect on New Zealand in 1956, when the surfriding film producer Bud Browne visited the country to show his film "Cavalcade of Surfing". At that time the only people interested in such a film were the lifesavers who went along to the Berkeley Theatre at Mission Bay in Auckland, to see how surfriding was done on the other side of the world.

There is no doubt that surfriding throughout the world developed rapidly after the introduction of the short hollow Malibu boards and grew even faster when the material polystyrene or foam plastic was used in surfboard construction.

During Christmas 1958 two American surfers, Bing Copeland and Rick Stoner, visited New Zealand and brought with them the first foam plastic 'Reynold Yater' shaped Malibu boards ever seen in New Zealand. They were guests of the Piha Surf Lifesaving Club of Auckland and with the club went down to the 1959 New Zealand Surf Lifesaving Championships at Oakura Beach, near New Plymouth, where they competed successfully in the paddle board event.

In 1960 at the New Zealand Surf Lifesaving Championships at Gisborne the effect of the visit by the Americans a year earlier was evident. It proved to be the first meeting of Malibu boards in New Zealand. Most of the boards at the Champs were nine to ten feet in length with wide rounded backs and pointed noses. This design was known as, 'The Pig Board'. Two other early board builders were Bob Ryan and Frank Wilkens, both of Auckland. Frank Wilkens is recognised as being the pioneer of factory made boards in New Zealand. His models were known as Plasticraft boards.

After New Zealand surfers of the early 1960's had developed their foam plastic boards to a practical stage, their next task was to find suitable beaches on which to use them. Piha Beach in Auckland and Mt Maunganui in the Bay of Plenty were two of the more popular surfing beaches at that time. But today perhaps New Zealand's most famous surf break would be at Raglan, about 60 kilometres west of Hamilton in the North Island. Early surfers knew Raglan as the beach where the waves travelled sideways to the land. Such a beach is now known as a point break. Due to Raglan's fame, there is some controversy over who was the first person to actually ride 'The Point'. It is believed that it was first bodysurfed in 1945. But Peter Miller claims that he first rode there on February 28th 1960, on a ten foot hollow board. Two of the earlier riders to visit and surf 'The Point' regularly were Mike Court and Campbell Ross, both from Hamilton.

In the early 1960's surfriding in New Zealand was developing faster than ever before and the influence from overseas surfing countries was considerable. Pop groups like the Beach Boys, were drawing the attention of teenagers towards the sport. The motion picture industry also helped in promoting surfriding, with a series of films about a young girl surfer called 'Gidget'.

So it was the Surf Lifesaving movement, 'Hollywood' and the short polystyrene Malibu surfboard that were some of the major influences on surfriding becoming the highly competitive worldwide business and sport that it is today.

*Surfer Mike Christensen*

| | |
|---|---|
| **All Black** | A member of New Zealand's top rugby-football team |
| **Aussie** | Australia or Australian |
| **Backblocks** | remote area |
| **Barrister** | lawyer who appears in court |
| **Bach** | holiday home |
| **Bird** | girl |
| **Biscuit** | a cookie |
| **Bludger** | someone who borrows but rarely returns the favour |
| **Bonnett** | hood |
| **Boot** | trunk |
| **Boowai or boo-eye** | the outbacks |
| **Booze** | hard liquor, the place where it is sold is the boozer, hotel or pub |
| **Bush** | the forest |
| **Caravan** | trailer for living in |
| **Cattle run** | farm or ranch for beef cattle |
| **Cheesed off** | to be fed up |
| **Chemist shop** | pharmacy |
| **Chillybin** | food and drink cooler |
| **Cobber** | mate — an Australian term widely used in New Zealand to refer to ones friend |
| **Cow Cocky** | dairy farmer |
| **Cocky** | any type of farmer |
| **Crook** | a criminal, or to feel sick |
| **Dag** | funny fellow |
| **Dairy** | shop selling milk, bread and groceries |
| **Dressing gown** | bath robe |
| **Feed** | a meal |
| **Flat** | apartment |
| **Footpath** | sidewalk |
| **Fortnight** | two weeks |
| **Freezing works** | slaughter house |
| **Fridge** | refrigerator |
| **Frock** | dress |
| **Fruiterer** | greengrocer |
| **Get cracking** | move |
| **Good screw** | good paycheck, good sex |
| **Grizzle** | complain |
| **Hardcase** | humorous but slightly offbeat |
| **Holiday** | vacation |
| **Jack up** | arrange |
| **Joker** | man |
| **Kerb** | curb |
| **Kiwi** | New Zealander or native bird |
| **Letterbox** | mail box |
| **Lift** | elevator |

# KIWI ENGLISH

Although naturally there are some regional variations, by and large New Zealanders and Australians use the same slang and colloquialisms as do other English speaking peoples. However Maori and Pakeha do use some words in a slightly different way than that to which Americans and or British visitors are accustomed. A few common examples are given below. The list is by no means exhaustive.

*Surfer Rangi King*

*Surfer Clint Day*

| | |
|---|---|
| **Lorry** | truck |
| **Mate** | friend as in "How are you Mate?" |
| **Ocker** | Australian |
| **Outback** | rural area |
| **Paddock** | field, meadow |
| **Pavement** | sidewalk |
| **Petrol** | gasoline |
| **Pissed** | drunk |
| **Pom** | Englishman |
| **Post a letter** | mail a letter |
| **Pram** | a baby carriage |
| **Pub** | bar, hotel |
| **publican** | hotel manager |
| **Quarter past** | quarter after the hour |
| **Quarter to** | quarter before the hour |
| **Queue** | line of people waiting for something |
| **Railway** | railroad |
| **Reel of cotton** | spool of thread |
| **Return ticket** | return trip ticket |
| **R.S.A.** | Returned Services Association equivalent to the U.S. Veterans of Foreign Wars |
| **Ring up** | call up |
| **Rubber** | eraser |
| **Scrounge** | obtain something for nothing |
| **Sheila** | borrowed from Australia meaning a woman |
| **She's right** | it's okay |
| **Shop** | store |
| **Shot through** | disappeared, gone away |
| **Shout** | buy drinks |
| **Skite** | loud mouth |
| **Smoko** | coffee break |
| **Solicitor** | non-court lawyer |
| **Spell** | rest period |
| **Station** | ranch |
| **Stiff Cheese** | bad luck, unlucky |
| **Sport** | friend as in "How are you Sport?" |
| **Stockyard** | corral |
| **Sweets** | dessert or candy |
| **Takeaway** | fast food eat out restaurant |
| **Tarmac** | airport parking area for aircraft |
| **Teem** | rain heavily |
| **Telephone Box** | telephone booth |
| **Too right** | yes indeed |
| **Tramp** | hike |
| **Varsity** | university. College to a Kiwi is High School. |
| **Wally** | a nerd or fool |

*Taranaki, North Island. Photo Mike Spence*

*Surfer Rangi King*

*Maungamaunu Marae*

# MAORI PHRASES

| | |
|---|---|
| ae | yes |
| Aotearoa | New Zealand (land of the long white cloud) |
| aroha | love |
| haere mai | welcome |
| haere ra | farewell |
| haka | dance |
| hakari | feast |
| hangi | oven, where food is cooked by heated stones |
| hau | wind |
| he aha te kupu maori mo | What is the Maori word for. . . |
| kahore | no |
| ka hore ahau e mohio | I dont understand Maori |
| ka pai te rangi ataahua | What a lovely day |
| kai | eat, food |
| ka pai | good or thank you |
| kauri | giant native forest tree |
| karekare | surf |
| kei whea a | where is |
| kia ora | good health |
| kowhai | tree with golden flowers |
| kumara | sweet potato |
| mana | authority, prestige |
| manuka | shrub, also called tea-tree |
| maoritanga | explanation meaning Maori culture |
| marae | ground used as meeting place |
| marama | moon |
| marena | marry |
| maunga | mountain |
| moa | large extinct native bird |
| moana | ocean |
| moko | face tattoo |
| motu | island |
| pa | stockade, fortified place |
| pakeha | European |
| papa | father |
| paua | large shellfish |
| pipi | small shellfish |
| pohutukawa | red flowering tree at Christmas time |
| poi | ball-swung to accompaniment of a song |
| ra | sun |
| rangi | sky |
| tai | sea or tide |
| takutai | coast |
| tane | male, husband |
| tangi | mourning |
| tapu | under religious restriction, forbidden |
| taro | plant cultivated for food |
| tena koe | hello |
| tiki | greenstone figure worn around the neck |
| toheroa | shellfish |
| tohunga | priest |
| tuatua | shellfish |
| tuatara | lizard |
| tui | native bird of New Zealand |
| ua | rain |
| utu | revenge |
| wahine | female, wife |
| wai | water |
| waka | boat |
| whaea | mother |
| whare | house, hut, shed |
| whenua | land |

*Top: Sunset. Photo Mike Spence. Above: Surfer Tim Barton*

### Types of Swell

There are two main types of swell that break on New Zealand shores. They are known as wind swells and ground swells. There are several theories as to what causes ground swells, which are the most favoured by surfers since they are even and well spaced and last the longer of the two types. Oceanologists believe ground swells are caused by a combination of factors, such as, ocean currents, tides and storms. When a storm rages out at sea, swells will radiate out from it and sometimes travel across thousands of miles of ocean. On the other hand, a wind swell is caused by strong fresh winds that blow a relatively short distance from the coast. This creates closely spaced swells which are normally lumpy in shape and inconsistent.

New Zealand experiences these two swells in varying degrees around its shores. The west coast receives a lot of wind swells, due mainly to the prevailing wind blowing across the Tasman Sea from the west. The east coast often receives ground swells from storms in the South Pacific Ocean.

### Types of breaks

There are four main types of breaks in New Zealand. They are the beach break, the reef break, point break and the river or harbour mouth break. The beach break is the most common type in New Zealand.

### The beach break

This type of wave breaks over a sand bottom. Just as the wind can alter the shape of a sandhill in a matter of days so can ocean turbulence alter the shape of beach break waves by shifting the sand banks around. For example, if the bottom develops a long gently sloping contour, there is a downward drag created at the base of the wave causing it to become thinner and slower moving; this type of wave is ideal for inexperienced surfriders due to its lack of force when breaking.

### The point break

The point break is generally considered to be the most consistent shaped wave type. It is formed when swells move along a peninsula or headland. Usually the bottom is comprised of lava rock or boulders which means the wave shape only alters as the tide moves in or out. On high tide a point break wave usually becomes slow breaking and flat whereas at low tide it becomes fast breaking and hollow. New

# NEW ZEALAND SURFING CONDITIONS

*Top Left: Murdering Bay Point, South Island. Photo Warren Hawke. Top Right: Reef. Photo Warren Hawke. Above: Surfer Ryan Matteer*

Zealand's most famous point break is Raglan situated fifty-six kilometres from Hamilton City, on the West Coast of the North Island. There are numerous other excellent point breaks throughout New Zealand.

## The reef break

This type of wave is formed when a swell breaks over a submerged reef which is comprised of solid rock, loose boulders or lava rocks. In countries like Australia, Hawaii and Bali, reefs are often made of sharp coral outcrops.

Reefs often break left and right, so natural and goofy foot surfers are accommodated on the same reef. Since reefs can be found a long distance from the shore line, waves can disappear altogether as they move into deeper water between the reef and the shore. This type of break can also disappear during tidal changes.

Some of the finest reef break surf in New Zealand can be found in the Taranaki area in the North Island. In this district the now extinct Mt. Egmont has created numerous lava reefs.

## River bar surf

Due to the silt that builds up at a river or harbour mouth, bars form that can create excellent surfing conditions. This type of break should be treated with some caution due to the currents and rips that are common near river mouths.

## Winds

Winds of any strength and from any direction will have some effect on the quality of waves. New Zealand often experiences quick changes in weather conditions, consequently surfriders and windsurfers usually become keen amateur weather forecasters.

## Beach hazards

Despite the reputation a beach may have for being safe it can develop holes and rips overnight. Rips or moving currents of water travelling along the shoreline are a common danger at many beaches and are caused by changing tides and surf conditions. Experienced surfriders save energy by paddling with rips to help them reach the point where the surf is breaking.

At all times treat New Zealand beaches with respect and you will reduce the possibility of being caught unawares.

# USING THE BEACH DIRECTORY

There are over 327 surfing locations listed in the following chapter. There are many times that many also known to exist or waiting to be discovered around New Zealand's coastline. It is hoped the following directory will go some way towards helping the enthusiastic travelling surfer to discover and enjoy some of those surfing breaks and perhaps even help spread them more evenly along that section of the coast where the swells are breaking. Wave height where indicated is given in the imperial measurement of feet only as surfers worldwide have been slow to use the metric equivalent.

Windsurfing enthusiasts will also find most of the following information of considerable assistance in predicting and finding ideal windsurfing conditions and locations.

The abbreviated terms used are as follows:

Off = Offshore wind
Acc = Nearest Accommodation
Loc = Location of surf break

*Surfer Shadar Edelmann*

# NORTH ISLAND LOCATIONS

# ALPHABETICAL CROSS REFERENCE TO NEW ZEALAND'S SURFRIDING LOCATIONS

*Rolling Stones, Mahia, North Island. Photo Mike Spence*

## SOUTH ISLAND LOCATIONS

*Photo: Evening Session Mangamaunu*

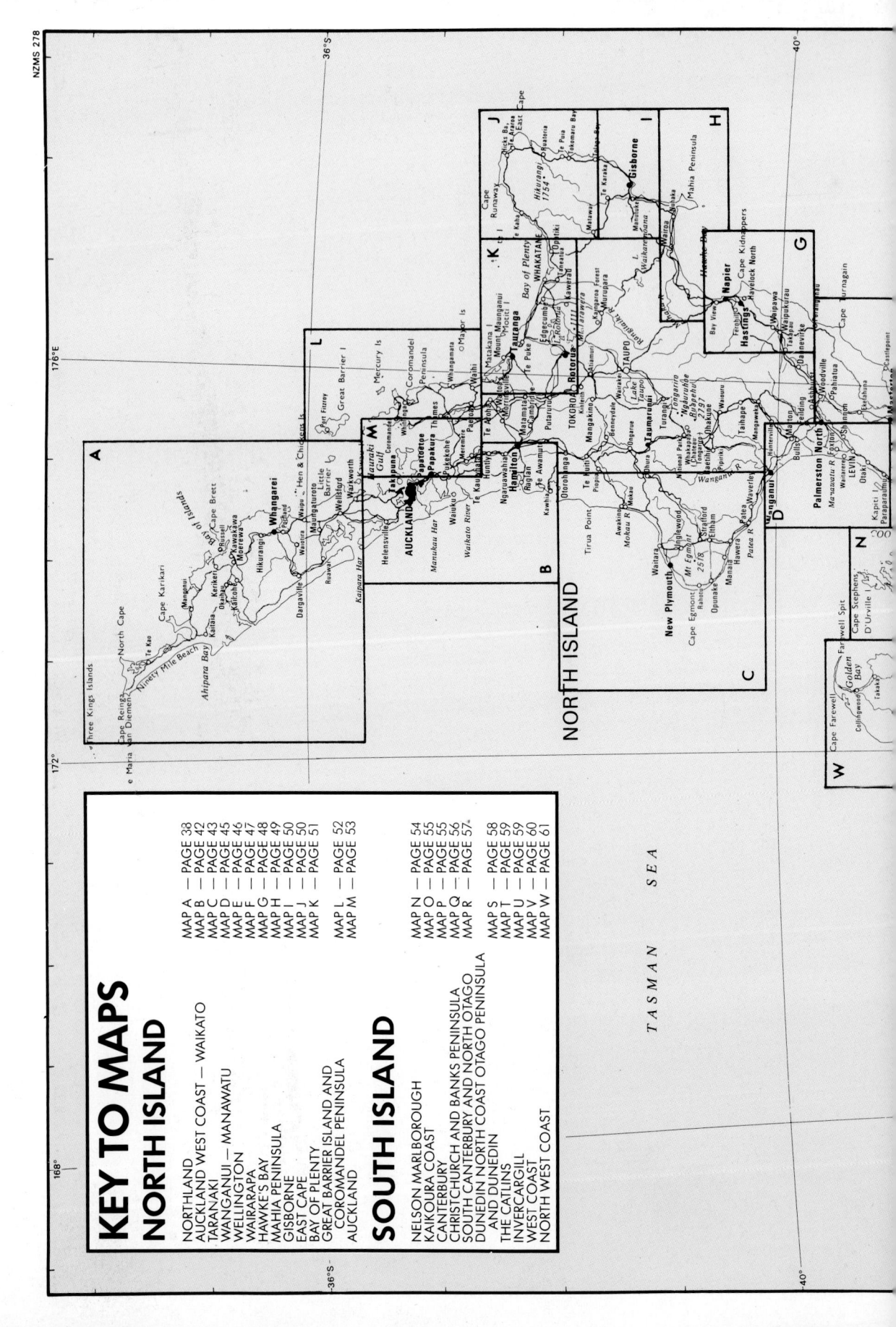

# KEY TO MAPS
## NORTH ISLAND

## SOUTH ISLAND

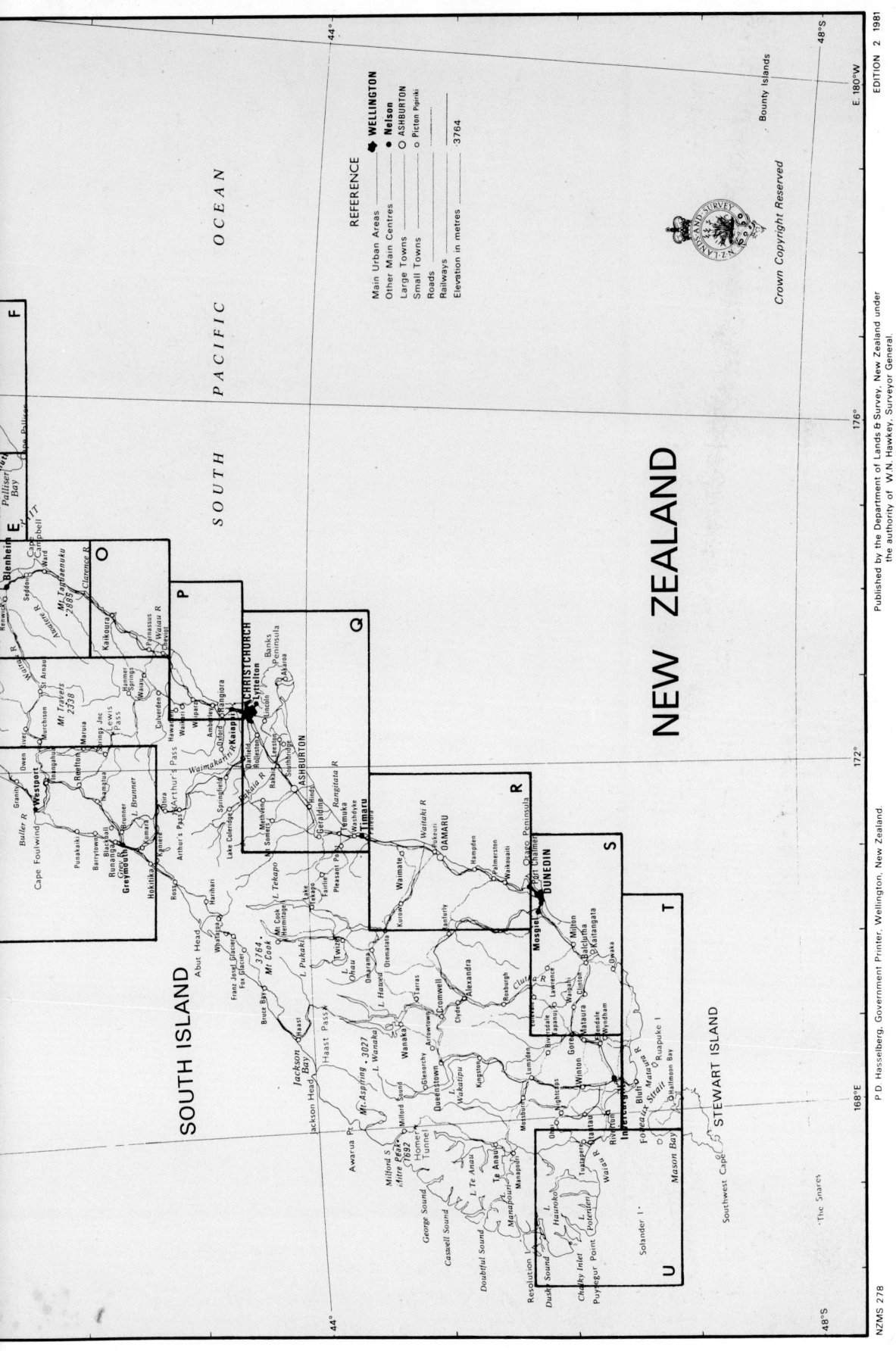

# NEW ZEALAND

## SOUTH ISLAND

### STEWART ISLAND

REFERENCE

| | |
|---|---|
| Main Urban Areas | ◆ WELLINGTON |
| Other Main Centres | ● Nelson |
| Large Towns | ○ ASHBURTON |
| Small Towns | ○ Picton Pipiriki |
| Roads | |
| Railways | |
| Elevation in metres | 3764 |

Crown Copyright Reserved

Published by the Department of Lands & Survey, New Zealand under
the authority of W.N. Hawkey, Surveyor General.

P.D. Hasselberg, Government Printer, Wellington, New Zealand.

NZMS 278

EDITION 2 1981

**1 Tokatu Peninsula**
Beach breaks.
Off. S.
Work on any tide.
Loc. 22kms East of Warkworth, drive to end of road.
88 kms from Auckland.
Acc. and garage at Warkworth & Leigh.

**1A Omaha**
Asst. good beach breaks.
Off. W.
Best at low tide.
Loc. approx. 22kms East of Warkworth.
Acc. and garage at Warkworth & Leigh.

**2 Daniels Reef**
Left and right reef break.
Fast breaking.
Off. N.
Best at high tide.
Loc. approx. 22kms NE of Warkworth, near Leigh.
Take Wonderview Road.
Acc. and garage at Warkworth & Leigh.

**3 Goat Island**
Beach break and reef needs a large swell.
Rocky.
Off. SE to SW.
Best at high tide.
Loc. approx. 24 kms NE of Warkworth.

**4 Pakiri Beach**
Good beach break.
Off. W.
Best from middle to high tide.
Loc. approx. 32 kms North of Warkworth.
Acc. and garage at Warkworth.

**4A Forestry**
Good beach break.
Off. W.
Asst. tides.
Loc. just south of Te Arai Point.

**5 Te Arai Point**
Beach break, fast breaking.
Off. W.
Best from middle to high tide.
Loc. approx. 48 kms North of Warkworth.
Acc. and garage at Warkworth.

**6 Mangawai Heads**
River bar and beach break.
Off. W.
Best from middle to high tide.
Loc. 28 kms South of Waipu.
Acc. and garage at Mangawai.

**7 Laings Beach**
Beach break.
Off. S.
Best at middle tide.
Loc. 19 kms South of Waipu.
Acc. and garage at Mangawai.

**8 Waipu Cove**
Good beach break.
Off. SW.
Best at middle tide.
Loc. 13 kms South of Waipu.
Acc. and garage at Waipu.

**9 Marsden Point**
Beach break.
Off. NW.
Best from middle to high tide.
Loc. 40kms South of Whangarei.
Acc. at Ruakaka, garage at Waipu.

# NORTH ISLAND
## NORTHLAND — MAP A

### 12 Sandy Bay
Good beach break.
Off. W.
Best at high tide.
Loc. 32 kms North of Whangarei.
Acc. and garage at Whangarei.

### 12A Whananaki North & South
Good beach breaks.
Walk over bridge across harbour
to south beaches.
Off. W.
Asst. tides.
Loc. 46kms NE of Whangarei.
Motorcamp on north side.

### 13 Mimiwhangata
Beach break.
Off. W.
Best at middle tide.
Loc. a few kilometres south of Helena
Bay.
Acc. and garage at Whangarei.

### 14-20 Seven unnamed good beach breaks
Off. W.
Best from middle to high tide.
Loc. from Mimiwhangata to Helena
Bay.
Acc. and garage at Whangarei.

### 21-24 Helena Bay to Bland Bay
Four beach breaks.
Off. W.
Best from middle to high tide.
Approx. 48 kms North of Whangarei.
Acc. at Oakura garage and Russell.

### 25 Russell
Russell beaches best on a large swell.
Off. W.
Good on all tides.
Loc. 248 kms north of Auckland.
Acc. and garage at Russell.
Deep sea fishing.

### 26-32 Taronui Bay, Tapuaetahi & The Ledge
Two left and right reef breaks at high
tide.
Two beach breaks, best at high tide.
Two left and right bomboras (large
breaks), best at high tide.
One left point break. Best at middle
tide.
Swells must be over 6 ft for these breaks
to work properly.
Off. SE to SW.
Loc. approx. 8 kms North of Kerikeri.
Acc. and garage at Kerikeri.
Access over clay roads.

### 10 Ocean Beach
Beach break.
Off. W.
Best at middle tide.
Loc. 40 kms from Whangarei.
Acc. and garage at Whangarei Heads.
Deep sea fishing.

### 11 Pataua
Right, river bar break.
Off. W.
Best from middle to high tide.
Loc. 32 kms East of Whangarei.
Acc. and garage at Whangarei.

### 33 Takou Bay, at Takou River Mouth
Left and right river bar break.
Consistent.
Off. W.
Best at high tide.
Access through a farm.
Loc. 13 kms North of Kerikeri.
Acc. and garage at Kerikeri.

### 34 Matauri Bay
Beach break, best on a large swell.
Off. W to S.
Best from middle to high tide.
Loc. 19 kms North of Kerikeri.
Acc. and garage at Kerikeri.

### 35-37 Wainui Bay
Several beach breaks.
Off. NW to SW.
Good on all tides.
Loc. 28kms North of Kerikeri.
Acc. at Whangaroa. Garage at Kaeo.

### 38 Tauranga Bay
Good beach break, best on a large swell.
Off. S.
Best at low tide.
Loc. 19 kms from Mangonui.
Acc. at Whangaroa. Garage at Kaeo.

### 39 Taupo Bay
Left and right beach breaks. Sheltered.
Off. W.
Best at middle tide.
Loc. approx. 16 kms from Mangonui.
Acc. at Whangaroa, Garage at Kaeo.

### 40-43 Paradise Bay or Matukahakaha
Four very good beach breaks.
Sheltered.
Off. S.
Best from middle to high tide.
Loc. approx. 8 kms from Mangonui.
Acc. at Whangaroa. Garage at Kaeo.

### 44 Taipa in Doubtless Bay
Left and right river mouth and beach break.
Off. SW.
Best from middle to high tide.
Loc. 5 kms East of Kaitaia.
Acc. and garage at Mangonui.

### 45 Tokerau Beach in Doubtless Bay
Beach break consistent.
Off. W.
Best from middle to high tide.
Loc. approx. 48 kms East of Kaitaia.
Acc. and garage at Mangonui.

### 46 Karikari Beach
Beach break.
Off. S.
Best at middle tide.
Access over sand and clay roads.
Loc. 40 kms from Awanui and 51 kms

*Photo Mike Spence*

from Kaitaia.
Acc. and garage at Awanui.

### 47 Ranganunu Harbour Bar
Beach break, best on a large swell.
Off. S.
Best from middle to high tide.
Access over swampy road and 3 km walk to beach.
Loc. 29 kms North of Awanui. Take the road to Kaimaumau.
Acc. and garage at Awanui.

### 48 Hauhora Harbour Bar
Very good left bar break.
Off. W.
Best at middle tide.
1 km walk from road.
Loc. approx. 32 kms North of Awanui.
Acc. and garage at Awanui.

### 49 Ngataki Beach and Paxton Point
Beach break consistent and exposed.
Off. SW.
Best from middle to high tide.
Loc. approx. 40 kms North of Awanui.

Turn right 2 kms past Ngataki township.
Acc. and garage at Awanui.

### 50-53 Great Exhibition Bay
Numerous beach breaks. Close out over 12 ft.
Off. W.
Best from middle to high tide.
Loc. opposite Ninety Mile beach, approx 48 kms North of Awanui.
Acc. and garage at Awanui.

### 54 Parengarenga Harbour Bar
Left and right harbour bar, exposed.
Off. W.
Best from middle to high tide.
Difficult access.
Loc. approx. 64 kms North of Awanui.
Acc. and garage at Awanui.

### 55 Tom Bowling Bay
Beach break.
Off. S.
Best at middle tide.
Clay road access.
Loc. 3 kms West of North Cape.
Acc. and garage at Awanui.

*Surfer Mark Kearns*

### 56 Spirits Bay
Beach break consistent.
Off. S.
Best at middle tide.
Loc. 16 kms West of North Cape and approx 88 kms North of Awanui.
Acc. and garage at Awanui.

### 56A Tapotupoto Bay
Good beach break.
Off. S.
Asst. tides.
Signposted from road to Cape Reinga.

### 57 Herangi Beach
Good beach break.
Off. SE.
Best at high tide.
Loc. near Cape Maria Van Dieman 88 kms North of Awanui. Poor access.
Acc. and garage at Awanui.

### 58 Twilight Beach
Beach break.
Off. E.
Best at middle tide.
Loc. near Cape Maria Van Dieman over the hill from Scott Point. Approx. 86 kms from Awanui.
Acc. and garage at Awanui.

### 59 Scott Point
Combination beach and point break, closes out over 7 ft consistent.
Off. N to NE.
Good on all tides.
Loc. 3 kms South of Cape Maria van Dieman.
Approx. 85 kms North of Awanui.
Acc. and garage at Awanui.

### 60 The Bluff
Left bar break.
Off. N to E.
Best at middle tide.
Loc. at the middle of Ninety Mile Beach, approx. 64 kms North of Awanui.
Acc. and garage at Awanui.

### 61 Waipapakauri Beach
Beach break consistent and exposed.
Off. E.
Best at middle to full tide.
Loc. approx. 8 kms East of Awanui.
Acc. and garage of Awanui.

### 62 Shipwreck Bay – Ahipara Bay
Good beach break, best on a large South swell. Sheltered.
Off. S to SW.
Good on all tides.
Loc. 16 kms West of Kaitaia and 358 kms North of Auckland.
Acc. and garage at Kaitaia.

### 63 Mukerau Beach
Good left beach breaks, Supertubes and Pines. Sheltered and closes over 8 ft.
Off. S to SE.
Best at low tide.
Loc. 2 kms West of Wreck Bay. Access by walking over sand and rocks from Wreck Bay.
If Wreck Bay is 2 ft, this beach will be 4 ft.
Acc. and garage at Kaitaia.

### PLEASE NOTE:

a
On a South swell, when Shipwreck Bay is 2 ft, Scott Point will be 8 ft and over.

b
From Herekino to South of Dargaville at Bayleys Beach there are over 150 kms of exposed beach breaks, working best on a small swell. Offshore easterly and poor access.

# AUCKLAND WEST COAST WAIKATO — MAP B

**64 Muriwai Beach**
Beach break, exposed.
Off. E.
Best at high tide.
Loc. 50 kms North of Auckland.
Acc. at Muriwai garage at Kumeu.
Surf club at the beach.

**65 Maori Bay**
Beach break, exposed.
Off. E.
Best at high tide.
Loc. 6 kms South of Muriwai Beach.
Acc. and garage at Henderson.

**66 O'Neills — Bethels Beach**
Beach break, exposed.
Off. E.
Best at high tide.
Loc. 8 kms South of Muriwai Beach.
Acc. and garage at Henderson.

**67 North Piha**
Beach break, exposed.
Off. E.
Best at high tide.
Loc. 40 kms East of Auckland.

**68 Piha**
Good beach break, consistent.
Off. E.
Best at high tide.
Loc. 40 kms East of Auckland.
Acc. at Piha. Garage at Titirangi.
Surf Club at the beach.

**68A Karekare**
Off. NE to SE.
Asst. tides.
Loc. turn off left before Piha.

**69 Port Waikato**
Beach, left reef, and river bar break.
Off. SE to NE.
Best from middle to high tide.
Loc. 40 kms West of Pukekohe
Acc. and garage at Pukekohe.

**70 Manu Bay — Raglan**
Very good left point break.
Off. SE to SW.
Good on all tides. Very hollow at low tide.
Loc. 8 kms West of Raglan and 56 kms West of Hamilton.
Acc. and garage at Raglan.

**71 Whale Bay — Raglan**
Very good left reef break.
Off. SE to S.
Good on half tide.
Loc. 9 kms West of Raglan.
Acc. and garage at Raglan.

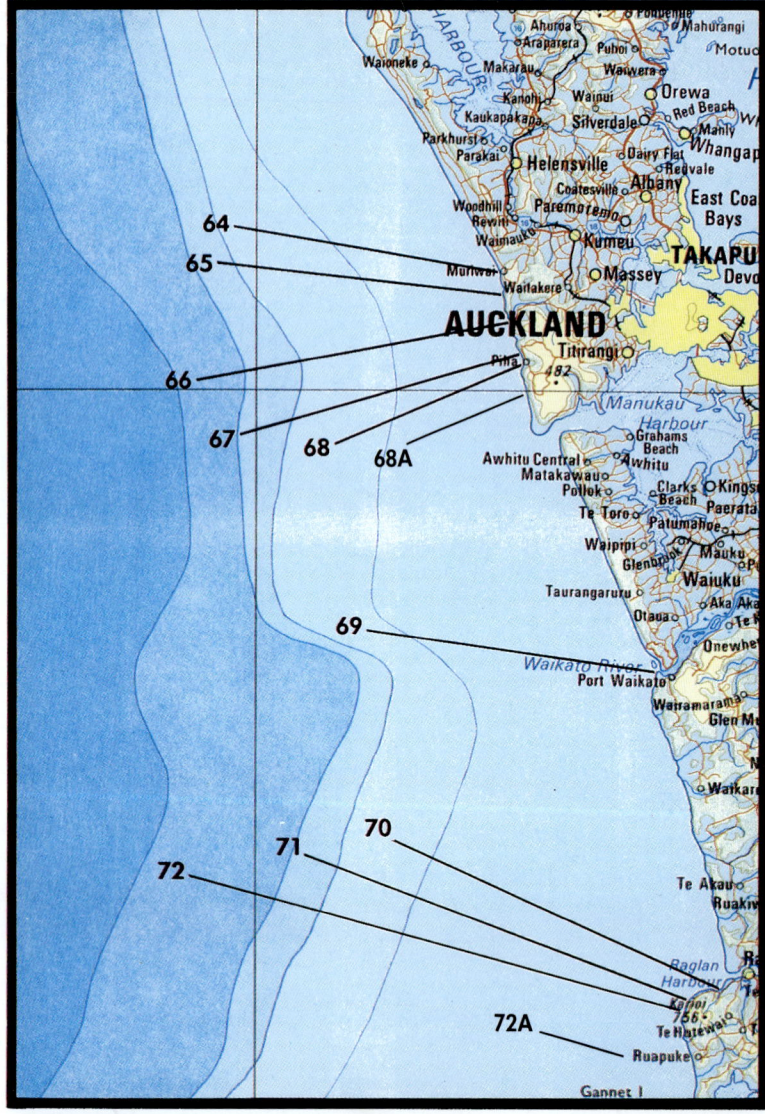

*Surfer Johnny Fenton*

**72 Indicators — Raglan**
Very good left point break.
Off. SE or light Southerly.
Best at low tide.
Loc. 10 kms West of Raglan.
Acc. and garage at Raglan.

**72A Ruapuke**
Check out if Raglan is small, you might get lucky, esp. on a SW. swell.

# TARANAKI AREA — MAP C

### 73 Marokopa
Good beach break.
Off. SE.
Best from middle to high tide.
Loc. approx. 48 kms North of Awakino.
Poor access.
Acc. and garage at Te Kuiti.

### 74 Awakino River Mouth
Very good left and right river bar
break.
Sheltered.
Off. SE.
Best at low tide.
loc. 76 kms South of Te Kuiti.
Acc. and garage at Awakino.

### 75 Waitara Bar
Left and right river bar break.
Off. SE.
Best at high tide.
Loc. 16 kms North of New Plymouth.
Acc. and garage at Waitara.

### 76 Bell Block
Left reef break.
Off. SE.
Best at low tide.
Loc. 10 kms North of New Plymouth.
Acc. and garage at New Plymouth.

### 77 Waiwakaiho
Very good left and right reef break.
Off. SE.
Best at high tide.
Loc. 6 kms North of New Plymouth.
Acc. and garage at New Plymouth.

### 78 Fitzroy Beach
Good beach break.
Off. SE.
Best at high tide.
Loc. at New Plymouth.
Acc. and garage at New Plymouth.
Surf Club at the beach.

### 79 East End and The Gap
Good left and right reef and beach
break.
Off. SE.
Best from middle to high tide.
Loc. at New Plymouth.
Acc. and garage at New Plymouth.

### 80 Belt Road or 'The Wedge'
Left reef break, needs strong swell.
Off. SW to SE.
Best at high tide.
Loc. northside of lee breakwater.

### 81 Paritutu and Ngamotu Beach
Beach break.
Off. SE.
Good on all tides.

Loc. 3 kms South of New Plymouth.
Acc. and garage at New Plymouth.

### 82 Back Beach
Beach breaks.
Off. E.
All tides.
Just South of Paritutu.

### 83 Oakura Beach
Beach break.
Off. SE.
Best at high tide.
Loc. 14 kms South of New Plymouth.
Acc. and garage of Oakura.
Surf Club at the beach.

### 84 Ahu Ahu Road
Good left and right reef break.
Off. SE.
Best from middle to low tide.

Loc. 3 kms South of Oakura.
Signposted.
Acc. and garage at Oakura.

### 85 Kumera Patch
Left reef break
Off. S to SE.
Best low to half tide.
Loc. 4 kms South of Oakura.
Acc. and garage at Oakura.

### 85A Rocky Rights and Lefts
Asst. reef breaks.
Off. NE to SE.
Asst. tides.
Loc. just South of Okato at end
of Paora Road.

### 85B Stent Road
Very good right reef break.
Off. NE to E.

43

Best middle to high tide.
Turn off just South of Warea.

### 86 Weld Road
Good right reef break.
Off. SE.
Best from middle to low tide.
Loc. 5 kms South of Oakura.
Signposted.
Acc. and garage at Oakura.

### 86A Anawhata Road, Oaonui
Right reef break.
Off N. to NE.
All tides.

### 87 Middleton Bay
Left and right reef break.
Off. SE.
Best from middle to high tide.
Loc. next to Opunake Beach.
Acc. and garage at Opunake.

### 88 Opunake Beach
Good beach break.
Off. NE to E.
Best from middle to high tide.
Loc. 43 kms West of Hawera and
64 kms South of New Plymouth.
Acc. and garage at Opunake.
Surf Club at the beach.

### 89 Desperation Point
Left and right reef break, holds up to
20 ft waves.
Off. NE to E.
Good on any tide, in a heavy swell.
Loc. 400 metres paddle from Opunake
Beach.
Acc. and garage at Opunake.

### 90 Sky Williams
Good left and right reef break.
Off. NE to E.
Best at high tide.
Loc. 5 kms South of Opunake.
Acc. and garage at Opunake.

### 91 Mangahume
Good left and right reef break.
Off. NE.
Best at high tide.
Loc. 5 kms out of Opunake.
Next to Sky Williams.
Acc. and garage at Opunake.

### 92 Greenmeadows
Good right reef break.
Off. NE to E.
Good on any tide in a heavy swell.
Loc. 8 kms South of Opunake. Farm
access.
Acc and garage at Opunake.

### 93 Patea River Mouth
Left river bar break.
Off. NE to E.
Best at high tide.
Loc. 27 kms South of Hawera.
Acc. and garage at Patea.

*Surfer Ernest Te Ruki 'showing how its done'*

# WANGANUI — MANAWATU AREA — MAP D

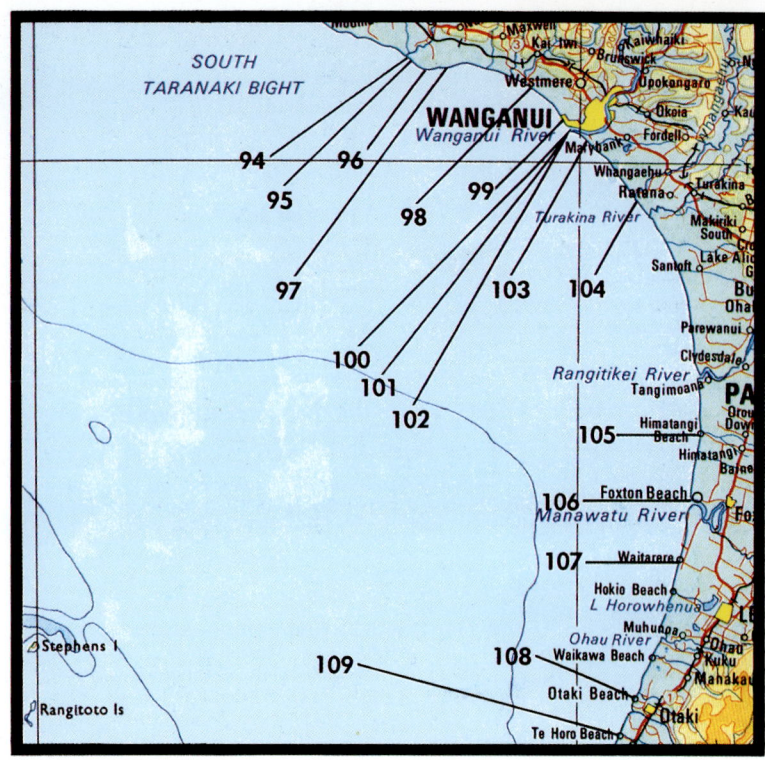

## 94 Nukumaru Rock
Right and left reef break.
Off. E to NW.
Good on all tides.
Loc. at Waitotara 32 kms North of
Wanganui. Turn off Jacksons Road for
Nukumaru Beach.
Acc. at Wanganui. Garage at
Waitotara.

## 95 'The Fences'
Good right reef break.
Off. NE.
Best at middle tide.
Loc. next to Nukumaru Rock 32 kms
North of Wanganui.
Acc. at Wanganui. Garage at
Waitotara.

## 96 The Point
Left and right reef break. Holds up to
12 ft waves.
Off. N to NE.
Best at middle tide.
Loc. 1 km walk from Wainui at
Waitotara, 32 kms North of Wanganui.
Acc. at Wanganui. Garage at
Waitotara.

## 97 Wainui
Right reef break.
Off. N to NW.
Best at high tide.
Loc. at Waitotara, 32 kms North of
Wanganui.
Acc. at Wanganui. Garage at
Waitotara.

## 98 Kai-Iwi
Beach break. Inconsistent.
Off. N to NE.
Best at high tide.
Loc. 16 kms North of Wanganui.
Acc. at Wanganui. Garage at Kai-Iwi.

## 99 Karaka Street
Beach break.
Off. N to NE.
Best at high tide.
Loc. at Castlecliff, Wanganui.
Acc. and garage at Castlecliff.

## 100 Rangiora Street
Beach break.
Off. N to NE.
Best at high tide.
Loc. at Castlecliff, Wanganui.
Acc. and garage at Castlecliff.

## 101 Morgan Street or The North Mole
Good beach break.
Off. N to NE.
Good on all tides.
Loc. at Castlecliff, Wanganui.
Acc. and garage at Castlecliff.

## 102 Wanganui River Mouth
Left river bar break. Dangerous currents
and river traffic.
Off. N to NE.
Good on all tides in a heavy swell.
Loc. at Wanganui River Mouth.
Acc. and garage at Wanganui.

## 103 South Beach
Beach Break.
Off. NE to E.
Best at high tide and on a heavy swell.
Loc. southern side of Wanganui River
Mouth at Wanganui.

## 104 Whangaehu River Mouth
Slow left river bar break.
Off. NE to E.
Good on any tide in a heavy swell.
Loc. 13 kms South of Wanganui and 6
kms North of Turakina.
Acc. and garage at Turakina.

## 105 Himatangi Beach
Beach break.
Off. E.
Best at high tide.
Loc. 37 kms West of Palmerston North.
Acc. at Palmerston North and garage
at Himatangi.

## 106 Foxton Beach
Beach break.
Off. E.
Best at high tide.
Loc 8 kms East of Foxton.
Acc. and garage at Foxton.

## 107 Waitarere
Beach break.
Off. E.
Best at high tide.
Loc. 19 kms NW of Levin.
Acc. and garage at Levin.

## 108 Otaki Beach
Beach break.
Off. E.
Best at high tide.
Loc. 3 kms West of Otaki.
Acc. and garage at Otaki Beach.
Surf Club at the beach.

## 109 Peka Peka
Beach break.
Off. SE.
Best at high tide.
Loc. 8 kms North of Waikanae.
Acc. and garage at Waikanae.

# WELLINGTON AREA — MAP E

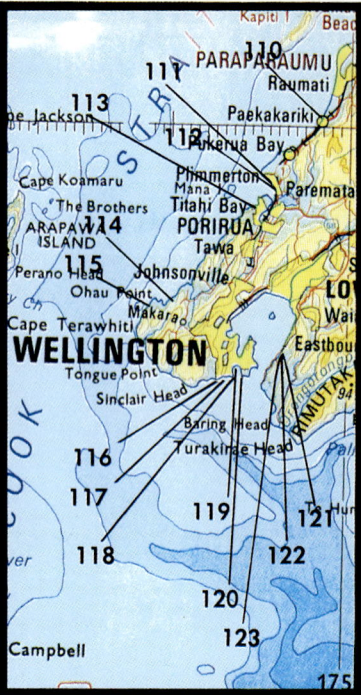

### 110 Paekakariki
Beach break.
Off. S. Best with no wind.
Loc. 40 kms North of Wellington.
Acc. and garage at Paekakariki.
Surf Club at the beach.

### 111 The Pa Point
Right point break. Best in a strong Northerly swell.
Off. SE.
Good on all tides.
Loc. 400 metres from 'The Pa'.
Acc. and garage at Paremata.

### 112 'The Pa'
Beach break. Best in a strong Northerly swell.
Off. SE.
Good on all tides.
Loc. 2 kms from Paremata and 26 kms North of Wellington.
Acc. and garage at Paremata.

### 113 Titahi Bay
Good beach break.
Off. SE.
Good on all tides.
Loc. 19 kms North of Wellington.
Acc. and garage at Titahi Bay.
Surf Club at the beach

### 114 Makara
Beach break.
Off. SE.
Good on all tides.
Loc. 16 kms West of Wellington.
Acc. and garage at Wellington.

### 115 Te Ikaamaru Bay
Beach break.
Off. SE.
Good on all tides.
Loc. 17 kms West of Wellington. Turn off Airforce Radio Station road, on the way to Makara. Farm access.
Acc. and garage at Wellington.

### 116 Island Bay
Right reef break best in a strong South swell.
Off. N.
Good on all tides.
Loc. 5 kms South of Wellington.
Acc. and garage at Wellington.
Surf Club at the beach.

### 117 Houghton Bay
Beach break.
Off. N.
Good on all tides.
Loc. 6 kms South of Wellington.
Acc. and garage at Wellington.

### 118 'The Bombora' — Lyall Bay
Right reef break. Holds up to 15 ft waves.
Off. N.
Good on all tides.
Loc. 6 kms South of Wellington.
Acc. and garage at Wellington.

### 119 Lyall Bay
Beach break.
Off. N.
Good on all tides.
Loc. 5 kms South of Wellington.
Acc. and garage at Wellington.
Surf Club at the beach.

### 120 'The Wall' at Lyall Bay
Good beach break.
Off. N.
Good on all tides.
Loc. 5 kms South of Wellington (at the Eastern end of Lyall Bay).
Acc. and garage at Wellington.

### 121 First Point — Eastbourne
Left reef to beach break.
Only in a heavy Southerly swell, best with no wind and at high tide.
Loc. 24 kms from Wellington.
Acc. and garage at Eastbourne.

### 122 Second Point — Eastbourne
Left reef to beach break.
Only in a strong Southerly swell, best with no wind and at high tide.
Loc. 24 kms from Wellington.
Acc. and garage at Eastbourne.

### 123 Third Point — Eastbourne
Left point break.
Only in a strong Southerly swell, best with no wind and at high tide.
Sheltered.
Loc. 25 kms from Wellington and a 2 km walk from the second point.
Acc. and garage at Eastbourne.

*Surfer Sam Johnson*

# WAIRARAPA — MAP F

## 123A Lake Ferry, Whatarangi and DeeDees
Asst. reef and beach breaks.
Off NE to NW.
Asst. tides.

## 124 Ning Nong Point
Good left point break.
Off. NE. Best in calm conditions, with a southerly swell.
Good on all tides.
Loc. 24 kms from Pirinoa and 64 kms from Featherston.
Acc. at Lake Ferry. Garage at Pirinoa.

## 125 Ning Nong Reef
Good reef break.
Off. Northerly. Best in calm conditions, with a southerly swell.
Good on all tides.
Loc. 32 kms from Pirinoa and 72 kms from Featherston.
Acc. at Lake Ferry. Garage at Pirinoa.

## 126 White Rock to Tora
Very good left and right reef and beach breaks.
Off. NW.
Good on all tides.
Difficult access 48 kms from Martinborough.
Acc. and garage at Martinborough.

## 127 Riversdale
Beach break.
Off. N to W.
Best at high tide.
Loc. 56 kms east of Masterton.
Acc. and garage at Riversdale.

## 128 Whareama
Beach break.
Off. N to W.
Good on all tides.
Loc. approx. 60 kms east of Masterton.
Turn off at Blairlogie onto the road to Riversdale.
Acc. and garage at Riversdale.

## 129 Christmas Bay
Beach break. Sheltered.
Off. N to W.
Good on all tides.
Loc. a walk over the hill from The Gap.
Acc. and garage at Castlepoint.

## 130 The Gap
Beach break.
Off. N to W.
Best at high tide.
Loc. 1 km South along the beach from Castlepoint.
Acc. and garage at Castlepoint.

## 131 Castlepoint Beach
Beach break. Coinsistent.
Off. N to W.
Good on all tides.
Loc. 69 kms east of Masterton.
Acc. and garage at Castlepoint.

## 132 'Slippery' — Castlepoint
Left reef break.
Off. N to W.
Good on all tides.
Loc 64 kms East of Masterton and 5 kms North of Castlepoint.
Acc. and garage at Castlepoint.

### 133 Owahanga

Beach break.
Off. N to W.
Good on all tides.
Loc. 32 kms East of Pongaroa and 93 kms East of Pahiatua.
Acc. at Pahiatua and garage at Pongaroa.

### 134 Akitio River Mouth and Reef

Good left and right river bar and reef breaks.
Off. Westerly.
Good on all tides.
Loc. approx. 37 kms East of Pongaroa and 80 kms from Pahiatua.
Acc. at Pahiatua and garage at Pongaroa.

### 135 Herbertville

Left and right reef to beach break.
Off. Westerly.
Good on all tides.
Loc. approx. 64 kms SE of Dannevirke.
Acc. at Dannevirke and garage at Pongaroa.

### 136 Porangahau River Mouth

Beach break.
Off. Westerly.
Good on all tides.
Loc. 53 kms south of Waipukurau.
Acc. and garage at Waipukurau.

### 137 Pourere Beach

Beach break.
Off. W.
Good on all tides.

Loc. 40 kms East of Waipawa.
Acc. and garage at Waipawa.

### 138 Blackhead

Right hand point break. Only in a heavy swell.
Access via farm roads.
Off. W.
Best at low tide.
Loc. 40 kms SE of Waipukurau. Acc. and garage at Waipukurau.

### PLEASE NOTE:

Some sections of the coast from Baring Head to Riversdale have yet to be properly explored for surf spots. Although there are a number of good breaks with access often through farm properties.

# HAWKE'S BAY — MAP G

### 139-40 Red Island

Left and right reef and beach break.
Sheltered.
Off. N to W.
Best at middle tide.
Loc. 6 kms South of Waimarama.
Acc. and garage at Hastings and Waimarama.

### 141-42 Cray Bay

Good left and right reef and beach break.
Sheltered.
Off. Westerly.
Best at middle tide.
Loc. turn off at Waimarama road.
Private farm access.
Acc. and garage at Hastings.

### 143 Waimarama

Good left and right reef and beach break.
Off. Westerly.
Best at middle tide.
Loc. 32 kms SE of Hastings.
Acc. and garage at Hastings.
Surf Club at the beach.

### 144-45 Ocean Beach

Left and right reef and beach breaks.
Off. Westerly.
Best at middle tide.
Loc. 11 kms North of Waimarama.
Acc. and garage at Hastings.

### 146 Raneika Beach

Left and right reef break.
Off. Westerly.
Good on all tides.
Loc. 6 kms North of Ocean Beach.
Acc. and garage at Hastings.

### 147 Te Awanga

Very good right point and reef break.

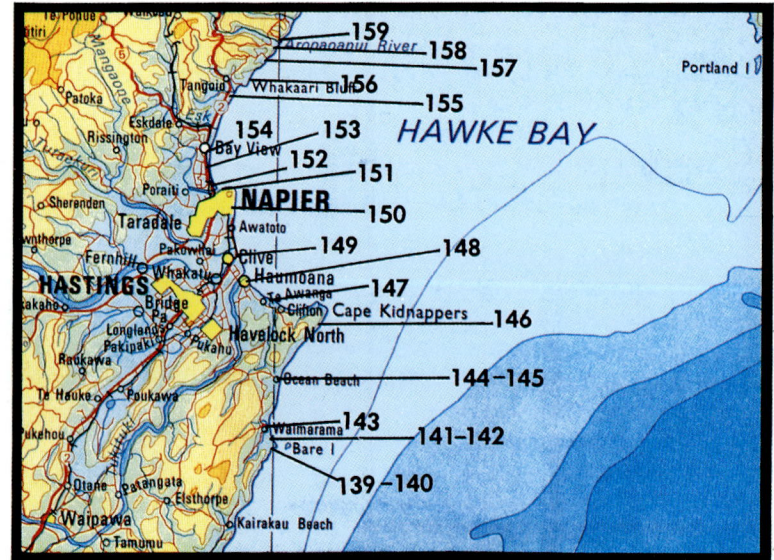

Off. SW.
Good on all tides with a S to E swell.
Loc. 16 kms East of Hastings.
Acc. and garage at Te Awanga.

### 148 Haumoana River Mouth

Left and right river bar break.
Off. W to SW.
Loc. at Haumoana.
Acc. and garage at Haumoana.

### 149 Tutaekuri River Mouth

Left and right river bar break.
Off. Westerly.
Best at middle tide.
Loc. 5 kms South of Napier.
Acc. and garage at Clive or Napier.

### 150 Marine Parade

Beach break. Undertow at the beach.
Off. Westerly.
Good on all tides.
Loc. at Napier.
Acc. and garage at Napier.

### 151 Hardings Road

Right point break. Best on a very heavy swell.
Off. SW to S.
Best at middle tide.
Loc. 2 kms NW of Napier, just South of the Napier wharves.

### 152 The Reef

Good left and right reef break.
Off. SW to S.
Good on all tides.
Loc. at the Southern end of Westshore Beach.
Acc. and garage at Westshore.

### 153 Westshore Beach

Beach break.
Off. SW to S.
Good on all tides.
Loc. 3 kms from Napier.
Acc. and garage at Westshore.
Surf Club at the beach.

### 154 The Gap, Westshore

Beach break.

Off. SW.
Best at low tide.
Loc. at Northern end of Westshore
Beach 11 kms North of Napier.
Acc. and garage at Westshore.

### 155 Tangoio
Beach break. Best on a large swell.
Off. N to W.
Best at middle tide.
Loc. 40 kms North of Napier.
Acc. and garage at Westshore.

### 156 Stingray Bay
Good right reef break. Closes out over 6 ft.

Off. N to W.
Best at high tide.
Walking access only.
Loc. 2 kms South of Waipatiki.
Acc. and garage at Westshore.

### 157 Tait's
Beach break.
Off. N to W.
Best at middle tide.
Loc. just South of Waipatiki. Poor access.
Acc. and garage at Westshore.

### 158 Waipatiki
Beach break.

Off. N to W.
Best at middle tide.
Loc. 40 kms North of Napier.
Acc. and garage at Westshore.

### 159 Aropaonui
Left reef break.
Off. N to W.
Best from middle to high tide.
Loc. 41 kms North of Napier.
Acc and garage at Westshore.

# MAHIA PENINSULA — MAP H

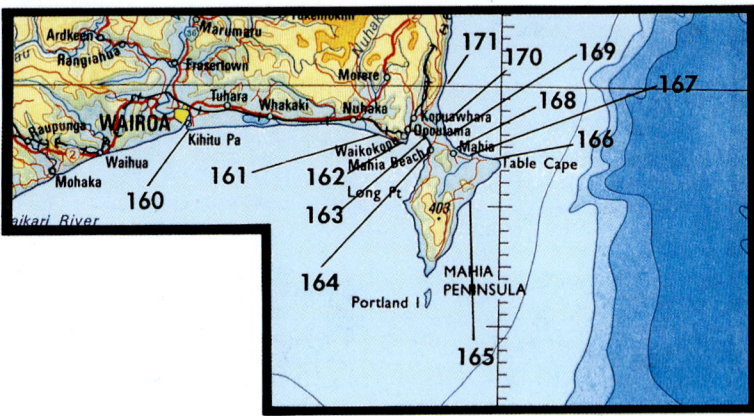

### 160 Wairoa River Mouth
Left and right river bar break.
Dangerous rips and currents.
Off. N.
Best at middle tide.
Loc. 2 kms from Wairoa township.
Acc. and garage at Wairoa.

### 161 Blacks Reef
Left and right reef break.
Off. N to NW.
Best at low tide.
Loc. 35 kms East of Wairoa.
Acc. at Opoutama. Garage at Nuhaka.

### 162 Point Annihilation — Waikokopu Bay — Rolling Stones
Right reef breaks.
Off. N to NW.
Best at low tide.
Loc. 40 kms East of Wairoa.
Acc. and garage at Opoutama.

### 163 Opoutama Beach
Beach break, 6 kms long.
Off. N to NW.
Good on all tides.
Loc. 43 kms East of Wairoa.
Acc. and garage at Opoutama.

### 164 Maiha Reef
Left reef break. Works best on a large swell.
Off. N to NW.
Good on all tides.
Loc. just South of Mahia.
Acc. and garage at Opoutama.

### 165 Diners Beach
Beach break.
Off. W.
Best at middle tide.
Loc. approx 24 kms East of 'The Spit'.
Acc. and garage at Mahia.

### 166 Several Unnamed reef breaks
Very good right and left reef breaks.
Off. W.
Best from middle to low tide.
Loc. approx 11 kms East of 'The Spit'.
Acc. and garage at Opoutama.

### 167 Unnamed reef and beach break
Beach break and good right reef break.
Off. SW to W.
Best at middle tide.
Loc. approx. 5 kms East of 'The Spit'.
Acc. and garage at Opoutama.

### 168 Three unnamed reefs
Good left and right reef breaks.
Off. S to W.
Good on all tides.
Loc. 2 kms East of 'The Spit'.
Acc. and garage at Opoutama.

### 169 The Spit
Very good left and right reef break.
Holds large swell.
Off. S to W.
Best from middle to high tide.
Loc. approx 16 kms from Opoutama.
Acc. and garage at Opoutama.

### 170 Mahunga Beach
Beach break and a good left point break at Northern end of the beach.

Off. S to W.
Good on all tides.
Loc. 57 kms East of Wairoa.
Acc. and garage at Opoutama.

### 171 'Last Chance' at Mahunga
Good point break.
Off. S to SW.
Best at half tide.
Loc. 2 km walk North of Mahunga or paying access via farm.
Acc. and garage at Opoutama.

Surfer Ian Fletcher

### PLEASE NOTE:
There are many unnamed breaks on the Mahia Peninsula and North to Gisborne. It is a very consistent area for swells and some breaks are still waiting to be discovered.

# GISBORNE AREA — MAP I

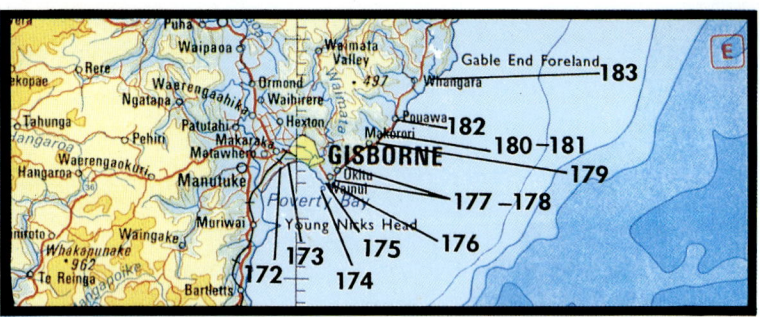

## PLEASE NOTE:

All garages and accommodation for this area are situated at Gisborne.

### 172 'The Pipeline' at Waikanae Beach

Good beach break.
Off. NE to NW.
Good on all tides.
Loc. 100 metres past Midway Surf Club.
2 kms from Gisborne City.

### 173 Waikanae Beach

Good left and right beach break.
Off. NE to NW.
Good on all tides.
Loc. 1 km from Gisborne City.
Surf Club at the beach.

### 174 Tuamatu Island — Inside and Outside break

Two good left reef breaks.
Off. NE.
Best at low tide.
Loc. 5 kms from Gisborne. Long paddle from Sponge Bay.

### 175 Sponge Bay

Good beach break.
Off. NE.
Best from middle to low tide.
Loc. 5 kms from Gisborne.

### 176 Tuahine Point

Good left reef break. Best on a large swell.
Off. NE.
Best at middle tide.
Loc. 5 kms from Gisborne. Long paddle from Sponge Bay.

### 177-78 Stock Route and Wainui Beach

Good beach breaks. Stock Route at Southern end of the beach.
Off. N to NW.
Best from middle to high tide.
Loc. 6 kms North of Gisborne.

### 179 Makarori Point

Very good right point break.
Off. NE to NW.
Best from middle to high tide.
Loc. 8 kms North of Gisborne.

### 180-81 North Makarori and Makarori Centre

Good left and right reef and beach breaks.
Off. NE to NW.
Best from middle to high tide.
Loc. 10 kms North of Gisborne.

### 182 Pouawa Beach

Good beach break. Works best on a small swell.
Off. NW.
Good on all tides.
Loc. 19 kms North of Gisborne.

### 183 Whangara

Good reef to beach break. Works best on a small swell.
Off. NW to SW.
Best from middle to low tide.
Loc. a short paddle down a creek from the main road, 28 kms North of Gisborne.

# EAST CAPE — MAP J

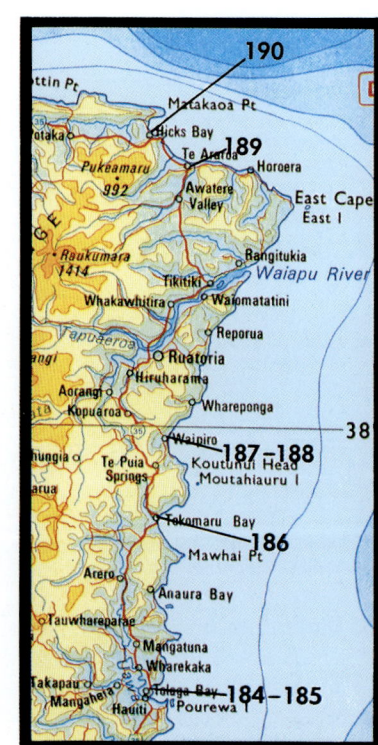

### 184-85 Tolaga Bay

Beach break and good right point break.
Approx. 2 kms from the beach. Needs a large swell.
Off. S to SW.
Best from middle to low tide.
Loc. 54 kms North of Gisborne.
Acc. and garage at Tolaga Bay.

### 186 Tokomaru Bay

Beach break exposed.
Off. S to SW.
Good on all tides.
Loc. 91 kms North of Gisborne.
Acc. and garage at Tokomaru Bay.

### 187-88 Waipiro Bay Area

Five good right point breaks and a beach break.
Off. S to SW.
Best at high tide.
Loc. 13 kms North of Tokomaru Bay, 104 kms. North of Gisborne.
Acc. and garage at Tokomaru Bay.

### 189 Horseshoe Bay

Good left and right point breaks.
Off. SW.
Best at high tide.
Loc. next to Hicks Bay 184 kms North of Gisborne.
Acc. at Hicks Bay. Garage at Te Araroa.

### 190 Hicks Bay

Beach break.
Off. SW.
Best at high tide.
Loc. next to Horseshoe Bay 184 kms North of Gisborne.
Acc. at Hicks Bay. Garage at Te Araroa.

## PLEASE NOTE:

There are several good reef and beach breaks known to exist from Opotiki to Te Kaha.

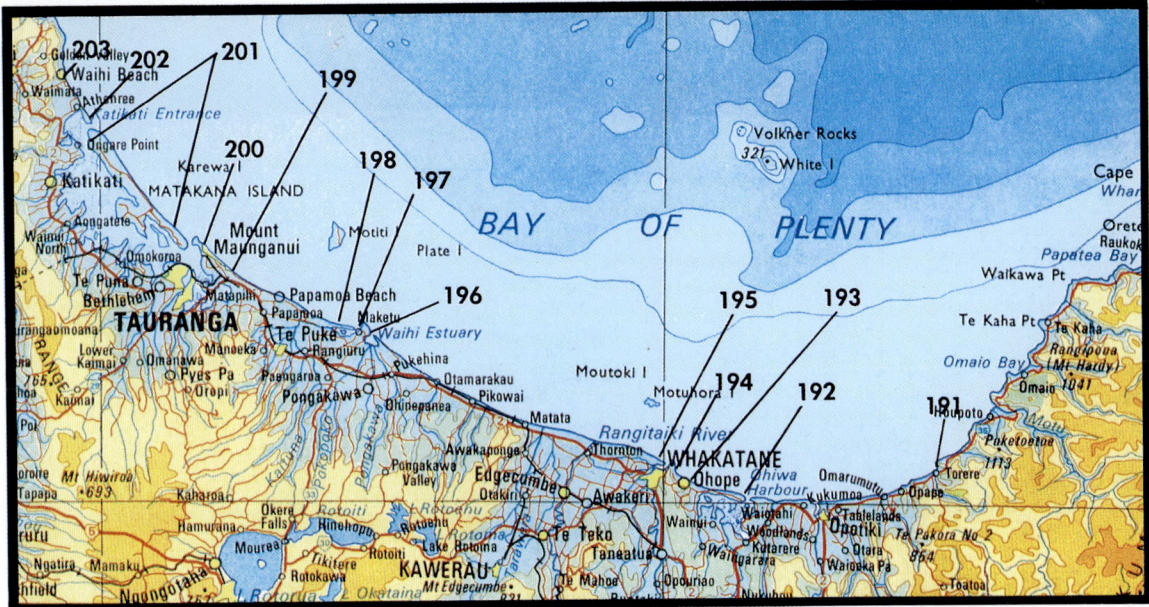

# BAY OF PLENTY — MAP K

**191 Torere Beach**
Very good right point break.
Only works on a strong North swell.
Off. S to SE.
Works on all tides.
Loc. 24 kms East of Opotiki.
Acc. and garage at Opotiki.

**192 Ohiwa — Port Ohope**
Good beach break.
Off. S. to SW.
Best at high tide.
Loc. 8 kms East of Ohope.
Acc. and garage at Ohope.

**193 Ohope Beach**
Good beach break.
Off. S to SW.
Best at high tide.
Loc. 6 kms East of Whakatane.
Acc. and garage at Ohope.
Surf Club at the beach.

**194 Ohope Beach — Western End**
Good left point break.
Off. S to SW.
Best at high tide.
Loc. 6 kms East of Whakatane.
Acc. and garage at Ohope.

**195 Whakatane Heads**
Good right reef and beach break.
Off. SE to SW.
Best at low tide.
Loc. 2 kms from Whakatane.
Acc. and garage at Whakatane.

**196 Newdicks Beach**
Beach break.
Off. S.
Best from middle to high tide.
Loc. 2 kms over hill from Maketu.
Acc. and garage at Maketu.

**197 Maketu Bar**
Right bar break.
Off. S.
Best at high tide.
Loc. 16 kms East of Te Puke.
Acc. at Maketu. Garage at Te Puke.

**198 Kaitura Cut**
Beach break.
Off. SW.
Best from middle to high tide.
Loc. 27 kms East of Mt Maunganui at mouth of Kaitura River.
Acc. and garage at Mt Maunganui.

**199 Tay Street**
Good beach break.
Off. SW.
Best at high tide.
Loc. 2 kms South of Mt Maunganui.
Acc. and garage at Mt Maunganui.

**200 Mt Maunganui Beach**
Good beach break.
Off. SW.
Best from middle to high tide.
Loc. 19 kms East of Tauranga.
Acc. and garage at Mt Maunganui.
Surf Club at the beach.

**201 Matakana Island**
Good beach break.
Off. SW.
Good on all tides.
Loc. At both ends of the Island, access by paddle or boat across entrance of Tauranga or Bowentown Harbour.
Caution, the safest time to paddle across is at the turn of the low tide.
Acc. and garage at Mt Maunganui.

**202 Bowentown**
Right hand sandbar.
Off. NW to SW.
Loc. South end of Waihi Beach near harbour entrance.
Acc. and garage at Waihi Beach.

**203 Waihi Beach**
Beach break.
Off. W.
Best from low to high tide.
Loc. 8 kms East of Waihi and 70 kms North of Tauranga.
Acc. and garage at Waihi.
Surf Club at the beach.

*North Island East Coast. Photo Mike Spence*

# GREAT BARRIER ISLAND

## and the COROMANDEL PENINSULA — MAP L

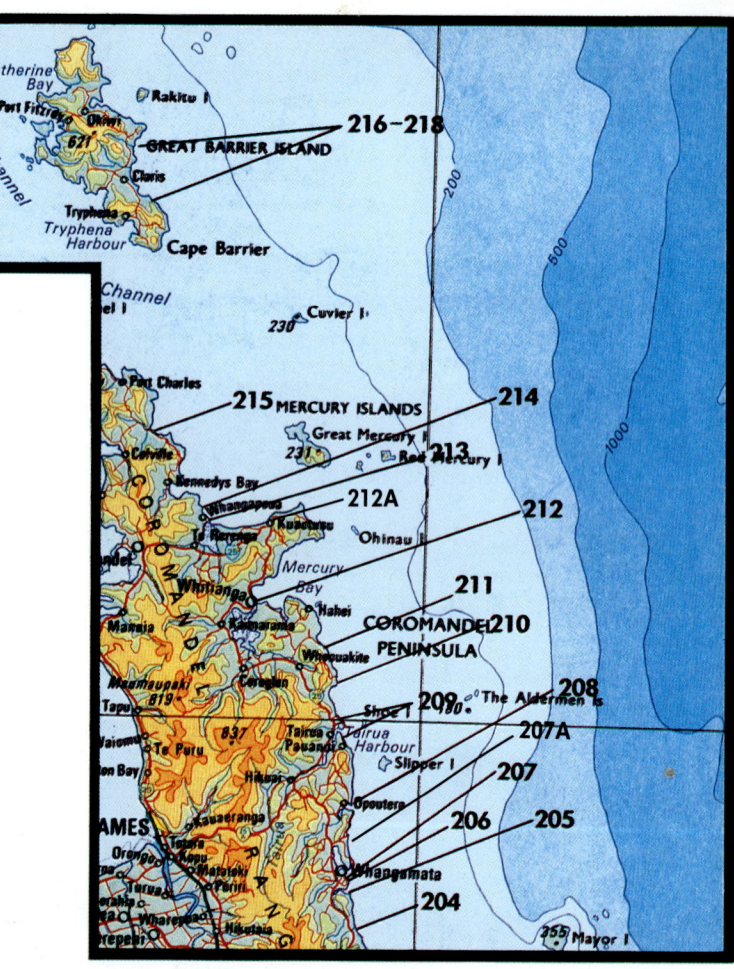

### 204 Whiritoa Beach
Beach break.
Off. NW to SW.
Best from low to middle tide.
Loc. 8 kms South of Whangamata.
Acc. and garage at Whangamata.

### 205 Whangamata Estuary
Right harbour bar break.
Off. NW to SW.
Good on all tides.
Loc. 3 kms South of Whangamata
township.
Acc. and garage at Whangamata.

### 206 Whangamata Beach
Good beach break.
Off. NW to SW.
Best from middle to high tide.
Loc. 30 kms North of Waihi.
Acc. and garage at Whangamata.
Surf Club at the beach.

### 207 Whangamata Bar
Very good left harbour mouth break.
Off. NW to SW.
Best at low tide.
Loc. 30 kms North of Waihi.
Acc. and garage at Whangamata.

### 207A Onemana
Beach break.
Off. NW to SW.
Asst. tides.
Loc. approx. 7 kms North of
Whangamata.

### 208 Opoutere Beach
Beach break.
Off. NW to SW.
Best from middle to high tide.
Loc. 30 kms North of Waihi.
Acc. and garage at Whangamata.

### 209 Tairua and Pauanui
Asst. beach breaks, separated by
a narrow harbour entrance.
Off. NW to SW.
Best from middle to high tide.
Loc. 64 kms North of Waihi.
Acc. and garage at Tairua and
Pauanui.

### 210 Sailors Grave
Good left and right reef and beach
breaks.
Off. NW to SW.
Loc. 5 kms North of Tairua.
Acc. and garage at Tairua.

### 211 Hot Water Beach
Beach break.
Off. SW to NW.
Best form middle to high tide.
Loc. 16 kms South of Whitianga.
Acc. and garage at Whitianga.

### 212 Whitianga
Beach break. Needs a large swell.
Off. SW to NW.
Best from middle to high tide.
Loc. 67 kms East of Thames.
Acc. and garage at Whitianga.

### 212A Kuaotunu
Right reef opp. boat ramp.
Off. SE to SW.
Asst. tides.

### 213 Whangapoua
Beach break.
Off. SW to NW.
Good on all tides.
Loc. 16 kms East of Coromandel.
Acc. and garage at Coromandel.

### 214 New Chums — at Whangapoua
Good left and right beach break.
Off. SW to NW.

Good on all tides.
Loc. a short paddle or walk North
around point from Whangapoua
Beach, 16 kms East of Coromandel.
Acc. and garage at Coromandel.

### 215 Waikawau Bay
Beach break.
Off. W.
Best from middle to high tide.
Loc approx. 80 kms North of Thames.
Acc. and garage at Coromandel.

### 216-218 Whangapoua, Okiwi, Awana Beach, Medlands Beach, Kaitohe Beach on Great Barrier Island
All good beach breaks.
Off. W to SW.
Various tides.
Loc. 80 kms East of Auckland by
boat or aircraft.
Accommodation available.

### PLEASE NOTE:
There are several other good breaks on
Great Barrier Island but only for the
more adventurous surfer.

# AUCKLAND AREA — MAP M

### 219 Orere Beach
Beach break works best on a large swell.
Off. W.
Best at high tide.
Loc. 32 kms East of Auckland.
Acc. and garage at Orere.

### 220 Waiheke Island
Various points, reef and beach breaks, needing a large swell to work properly.
Off. W.
Best at high tide.
Loc. 6 kms off Auckland's coast by ferry boat.
Acc. at Waiheke Island.

### 221 Takapuna — North Reef
Beach break best on a large swell.
Inconsistent.
Off. W.
Best at high tide.
Loc. 8 kms North of Auckland City.
Acc. and garage at Takapuna.

### 222 Takapuna and Milford Beach
Reef and beach breaks. Inconsistent.
Off. W.
Best at high tide.
Loc. 5 kms North of Takapuna.
Acc. and garage at Auckland.

### 223 Red Beach
Beach break. Inconsistent.
Off. W.
Best at middle tide.
Loc. 38 kms North of Auckland.
Acc. at Red Beach. Garage at Silverdale.
Surf Club at the beach.

### 224 Orewa Beach
Beach break. Inconsistent.
Off. W.
Best at middle tide.
Loc. 38 kms North of Auckland.
Acc. at Orewa. Garage at Silverdale.

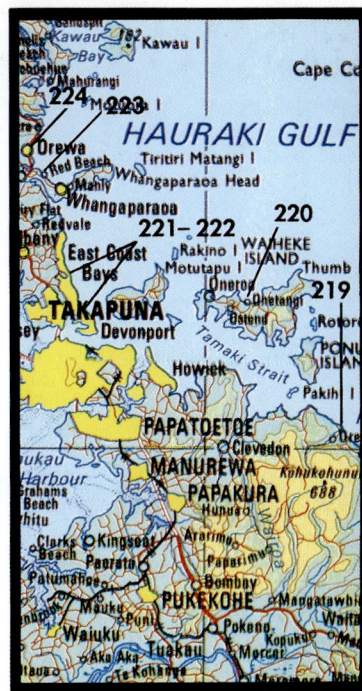

*Surfer Shaydar Edelmann*

# SOUTH ISLAND

## NELSON —MARBOROUGH AREA — MAP N

### 225 The Cut - At Nelson Harbour
Good right reef break.
Off. SE.
Best from middle to low tide on a North swell.
Loc. at the entrance to Nelson Harbour and requires 1 km paddle to reach it.
Acc. and garage at Nelson.

### 226 Schnappers Point
Good right point break, exposed.
Off. E.
Best from middle to low tide.
Loc. approx 11 kms NE of Nelson.
Acc. and garage at Nelson.

### 227 Delaware Bay
Good beach break.
Off. S.
Best from middle to low tide.
Loc. 24 kms NE of Nelson.
Acc. and garage at Nelson.

### 228 Delaware Bay Point
Good left point break beware of strong rip from a tidal river.
Off. S.
Best from middle to low tide.
Loc. at Western end of Delaware Bay.
Acc. and garage at Nelson.

### 229 Whangamoa
River bar break.
Off. S to SE.
Tide varies with sandbars.
Loc. approx. 40 kms from Nelson.
Acc. and garage at Nelson.

### 230 Robin Hood Bay
Beach break.
Off. NW.
Tide varies with sandbars in a south swell.
Loc. approx. 20 kms NE of Blenheim.
Acc. and garage at Blenheim.

### 231 Whites Bay
Beach break.
Off. NW.
Best at high tide.
Loc. 16 kms NE of Blenheim.
Acc. and garage at Blenheim.

### PLEASE NOTE:
The Nelson area is heavily dependent on big north swells from the Tasman Sea and is consequently not very consistent. When the swell is running however the waves are of good quality. The Marlborough area's potential is only partly known but it does get a lot of swell due to its close proximity to Cook Strait. There are probably rideable spots southeast of Blenheim at White Bluffs and in behind Lake Grassmere.

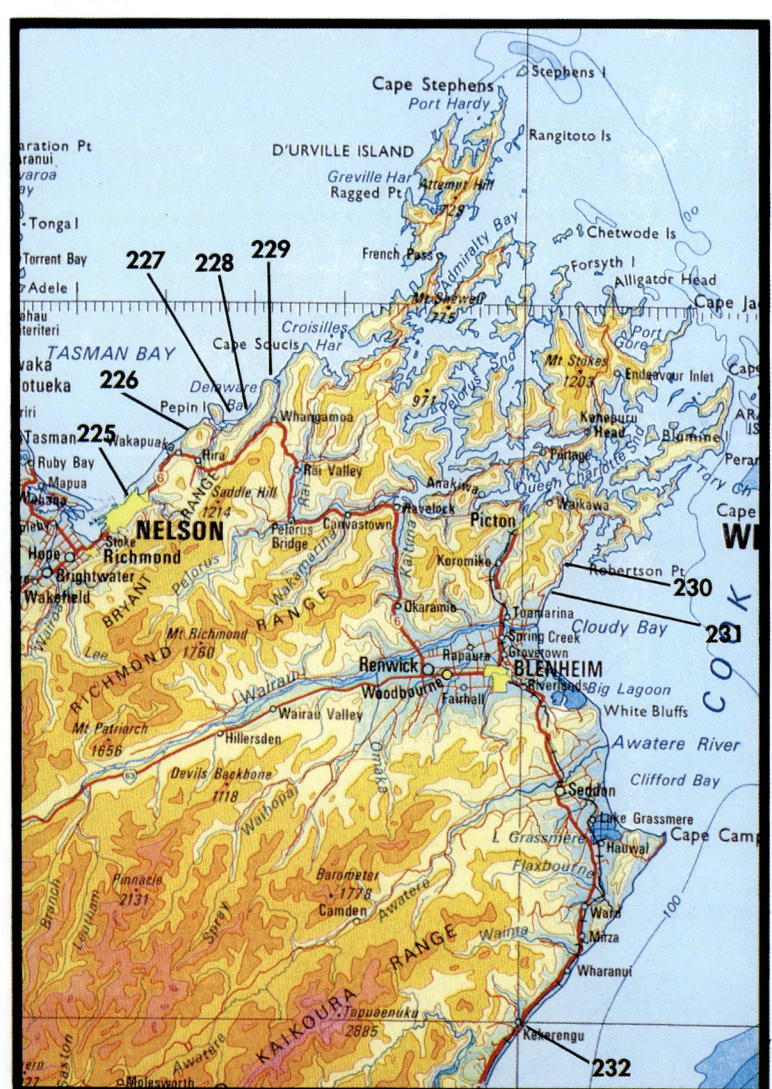

## KAIKOURA COAST — MAP 0

### 232 Kekerengu
Small right point break.
Off. W.
Best from middle to high tide.
Loc. approx. 56 kms North of Kaikoura.
Acc. and garage at Kaikoura.

### 233 Clarence
Right point, consistent.
Off. S.
Tide depends on swell size.
Loc. north end of aerodrome.
Acc. and garage at Kaikoura.

### 234 Waipapa Bay
Beach break.
Off. NE to NW. These winds are onshore at Mangamaunu.

Best from middle to high tide.
Loc. 32 kms North of Kaikoura.
Acc. and garage at Kaikoura.

### 235 Blue Duck Stream
Beach break.
Off. SW to NW.
Good on all tides.
Loc. just North of Mangamaunu.
Acc. and garage at Kaikoura.

### 236 Mangamaunu
Very good right point break, consistent.
Off. SW to NW.
Good on all tides.
Loc. 16 kms North of Kaikoura.
Acc. and garage at Kaikoura.

### 237 Meatworks
Beach break, consistent.
Off. W.
Best at low tide.
Loc. 2 kms South of Mangamaunu.
Acc. and garage at Kaikoura.

### 238 Kahutara
Right point break.
Off. NW to W.
Best at low tide on a south swell.
Loc. 18 kms South of Kaikoura.
Acc. and garage at Kaikoura.

### 239 Oaro
Off. NW to SW.
Tide varies with sandbars.
Loc. 24 kms South of Kaikoura.
Acc. and garage at Kaikoura.

### PLEASE NOTE:
The Kaikoura Coast has three of the best point breaks in the country and as a result can get crowded especially at weekends. The area is open to any swell and is therefore quite consistent throughout the year, but it's better from March to May. Check out whale watch-ing at Kaikoura if no swell.

# CANTERBURY —MAP P

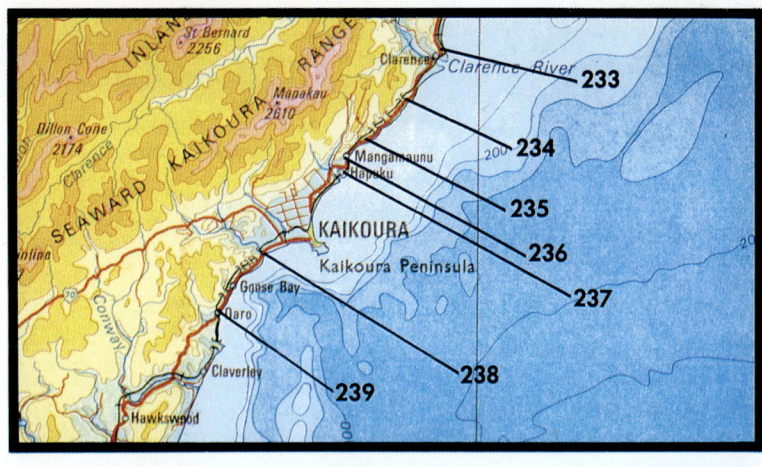

### 240 Gore Bay
Beach break.
Off. NW to SW.
Loc. 15 kms east of Cheviot.
Acc. and garage at Cheviot.

### 241 Port Robinson
Right point break.
Off. W. To SW.
Best at high tide.
Loc. 5 kms South of Gore Bay.
Acc. and garage at Cheviot.

### 242 Fields
Right point and beach break.
Off. NW to SW.
Point at high tide, beach at low tide.
Loc. 3 kms North of Motunau Beach.
Acc. and garage at Motunau.

### 243 Motunau Beach
Beach break and left point at the west end of the beach.
Off. N to NE.
Best at high tide on a south swell.
Loc. 80 kms North of Christchurch.
Acc. and garage at Motunau.

### 244 Midshore Bay
Left point.
Off. N.
Best at high tide.
Loc. 25 kms east of Waipara.
Acc. and garage at Waipara.

### 245 Leithfield Beach
Beach break.
Off. NW to W.
Best at low tide.
Loc. 42 kms North of Christchurch.
Acc. and garage at Leithfield.

### 246 Waikuku Beach
Beach break.
Off. NW to SW.
Tide varies with sandbars.
Loc. 29 kms North of Christchurch.
Acc. and garage at Leithfield.

### 247 Kairaki Beach
Beach break.
Off. NW to SW.
Tide varies with sandbars.
Loc. 18 kms North of Christchurch.
Acc. and garage at Kaiapoi.

'Another empty South Island wave...'

# CHRISTCHURCH & BANKS PENINSULA — MAP Q

### 248 New Brighton Beach
Beach break.
Off. W to SW.
Tide varies with sandbars.
Loc. 8 kms from Christchurch.
Acc. and garage at New Brighton.

### 249 Sumner Bar
River bar break.
Off. W to SE.
Tide varies with sandbars.
Loc. 8 kms from Christchurch.
Acc. and garage at Sumner.

### 250 Scarborough
Beach break.
Off. W to SE.
Best three hours before and two hours after high tide.
Loc. 9 kms from Christchurch.
Acc. and garage at Sumner.

### 251 Taylors Mistake
Beach break.
Off. SW to NW.
Good on all tides.
Loc. 5 kms from Sumner.
Acc. and garage at Sumner.

### 252 Banks Peninsula
Raupo, Stony, Hickery & Gough Bays.
All beach breaks.
Off. different for each bay.
Loc. approx 72 kms South of Christchurch.
Acc. and garage at Little River.

### 253 Te Oka Bay
Beach break.
Off. NW to E.
Best at low tide.
Loc. 10 kms from Magnet Bay.
Acc. and garage at Little River.

### 254 Magnet Bay
Good left point break.
Off. NE.
Best at low tide.
Loc. approx 16 kms from Little River.
Acc. and garage at Little River.

### PLEASE NOTE:
The Canterbury area is not renowned for top quality surf, but if you are keen and prepared to travel you shouldn't be disappointed.

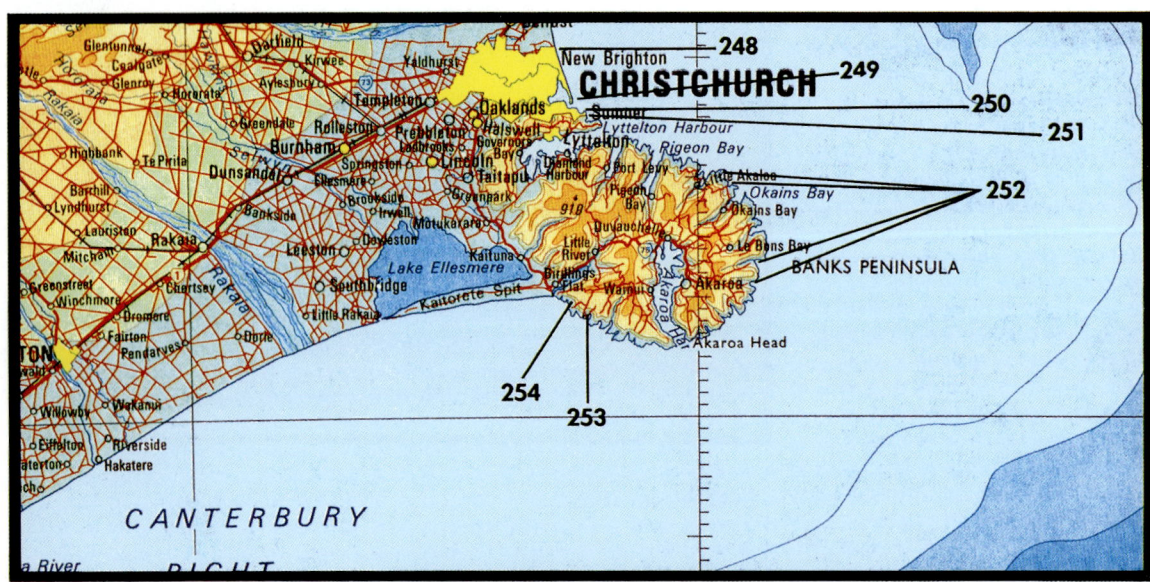

# SOUTH CANTERBURY AND NORTH OTAGO — MAP R

### 255 Patiti Point
Left reef break.
Off. W.
Best at high tide.
Loc. at Timaru.
Acc. and garage at Timaru.

### 256 Jacks Point
Left and right reef break.
Off. SW to W.
Best at high tide.
Loc. 3 kms South of Timaru. Turn off highway at Scarborough Road.
Acc. and garage at Timaru.

### 257 Lighthouse Reef
Left and right beach break.
Off. W.
Best at high tide, inconsistent.
Loc. ½ km South of Jacks.
Acc. and garage at Timaru.

### 258 Tuhawaiki Point
Right point break.
Off. W to SW.
Best at high tide on a North swell.
Loc. 2 km walk South of Jacks.
Acc. and garage at Timaru.

### PLEASE NOTE:
The Timaru area has some of the heaviest waves in the South Island and is therefore not recommended for beginners.

### 259 Crossroads
Right point break.
Off. W.
Best at low tide on a large South swell.
Loc. 10 kms South of Oamaru.
Acc. and garage at Kakanui.

### 260 Kakanui River Mouth
River bar break.
Off. NW to SW.
Tide varies with sandbars.
Loc. at South Kakanui.
Acc. and garage at Kakanui.

### 261 Campbells Bay
Left point and beach break.
Off. NW.
Best at high tide.
Loc. 13 kms South of Oamaru.
Acc. and garage at Maheno.

### 262 All Day Bay to Wainakarua River Mouth
A series of small point reef and beach breaks.
Off. NW to SW.

Tide varies with location.
Loc. South of Kakanui.
Acc. and garage at Kakanui.

### 263 Moeraki
Beach and right reef break.
Off. W to SW.
Best at high tide on a North swell.
Acc. and garage at Moeraki.

### 264 Lighthouse or 'Spot C'
Left point and reef break.
Off. NW to NE.
Best at low tide.
Loc. 5 kms South of Moeraki. Farm access.
Acc. and garage at Moeraki.

### 265 Shag Beach
Right reef and beach break.
Off. NW to SW.
Best at high tide.
Loc. on State Highway 1.
Acc. and garage at Palmerston.

**PLEASE NOTE:**

The North Otago coastline has considerable potential and is worth checking out. The area South of Oamaru in particular has some very good breaks.

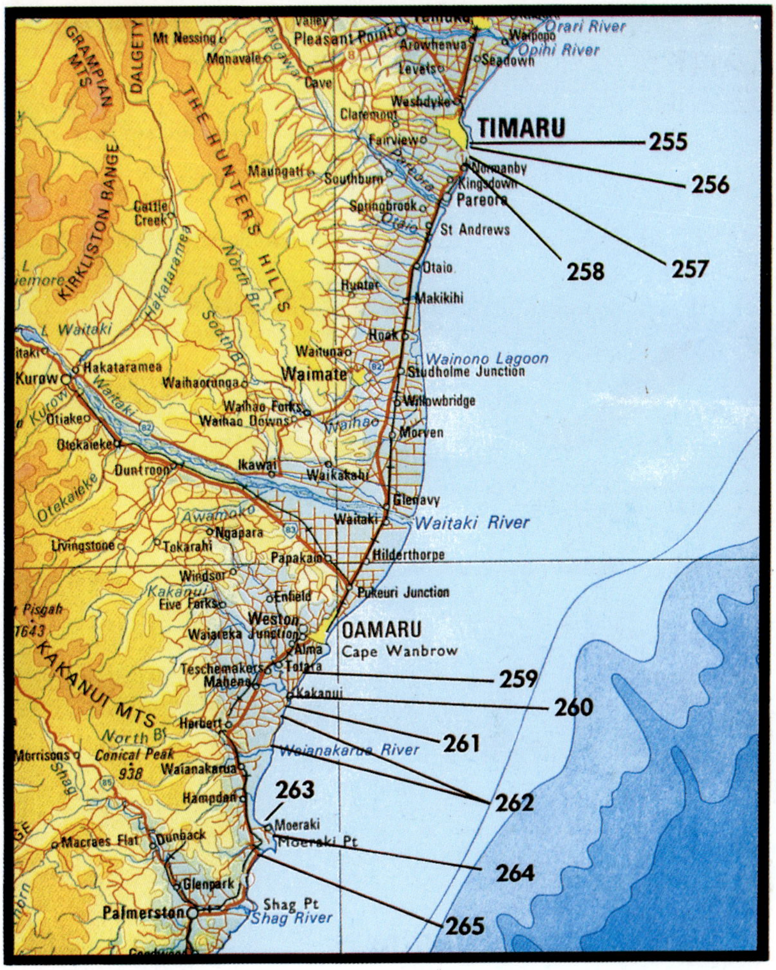

# DUNEDIN NORTH COAST — MAP S

**PLEASE NOTE:**
Accommodation and garages are plentiful in the Dunedin area.

### 266 'Pipeline'
Good river bar break.
Off. SW to SE.
Best at low tide.
Loc. 42 kms North of Dunedin — at the mouth of the Waikouaiti River.

### 267 Karitane Point
Heavy right point break.
Off. S.
Best at high tide on a north or heavy swell.
Loc. 42 kms north of Dunedin.

### 268 Possums Reef
Left reef break.
Off. NW to W.
Best at high tide on a NE to E swell.
Loc. 2 kms North of Warrington through farm.

### 269 Warrington
Beach and left reef break.
Off. SW.
Best at high tide.
Loc. 24 kms North of Dunedin.

### 270 Potato Patch
Right point break.
Off. SW to SE.
Best at low tide.
Loc. at Purakanui 30 kms North of Dunedin.

### 271 Murdering Bay
Right point break.
Off. SE.
Best at low tide.
Loc. 25 kms North of Dunedin.

### 272 Aramoana Spit
Good beach break.
Off. SW.
Best at low tide.
Loc. 21 kms North of Dunedin.

**PLEASE NOTE:**

This area of Dunedin does not break often but can be well worth the wait, with the 'Spit' being the most consistent.

# OTAGO PENINSULA — MAP S

### 273 Pipikaretu
Good beach break and right point break.
Off. SW.
Best at high tide.
Loc. approx. 29 kms North of Dunedin.

### 274 Allans Beach
Beach break — heavy rips.
Off. NE to NW.
Tide varies with sandbars.
Loc. East of Portobello.

### 275 Sandfly Bay
Beach break.
Off. NE to NW.
Best at low tide on a small south swell.
Loc. off Highcliff Road.

### 276 Smaills Beach
Beach break.
Off. NE.
Best from middle to low tide.
Loc. 8 kms East of Dunedin.

### 277 Tomahawk Beach
Beach break.
Off. NE to NW.
Tide varies with sandbars.
Loc. East of Dunedin.

# DUNEDIN — MAP S

### 278 St Kilda Beach
Heavy beach break.
Off. NE to NW.
Best tide varies with sandbars.
Loc. SE of Dunedin.
Surf Club at the beach.

### 279 Middle Beach at Moana Rua
Heavy beach break.
Off. N to NW.
Best from middle to high tide.
Loc. between St Kilda and St Clair
beaches.

### 280 St Clair
Beach and right point break.
Off. N to NW.
Best from middle to high tide.
Loc. South of Dunedin.
Surf Club at the beach.

### 281 Blackhead
Beach break.
Off. NE to NW.
Best at low tide.
Loc. 8 kms South of St Clair.

### 282 Brighton
Right point break.
Off. W to NW.
Best at low tide.
Loc. 19 kms South of Dunedin.
Acc. and garage at Brighton.

### 283 Cob Cottage to Kuri Bush
Reef to beach breaks.
Off. NW to SW.
Tide varies with sandbars.
Loc. between Brighton and Taieri
Mouth.

### 284 Taieri Mouth
Beach and river bar break.
Off. NW to SW.
Best at low tide.
Loc. 35 kms South of Dunedin.
Acc. and garage at Taieri Mouth.

### 285 Bob's Beach
Right point break.
Off. SW to NW.
Best at low tide.
Loc. approx. 8 kms South of Taieri
Mouth.

**PLEASE NOTE:**

There are other surf beaches on the
peninsula but they are rarely surfed. The
ones mentioned can be good but are
vulnerable to strong rips and heavy
swells.

**PLEASE NOTE:**

The Dunedin area has some of the best
beach breaks in the country, being fast
and powerful. The water is cold but very
clear and clean and flat days are rare.
The best time of the year is January to
May when the weather isn't quite so
changeable.

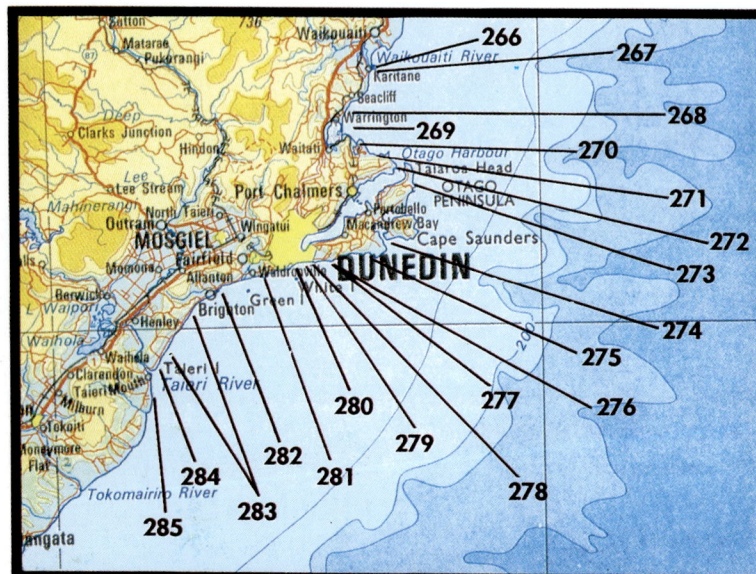

*'Somewhere along the South Coast...'*

# THE CATLINS — MAP T

### 286 Kaka Point to Nugget Point
Beach breaks.
Off. W to SW.
Various tides.
Loc. SE of Balclutha.

### 287 Cannibal Bay, Catlins River Mouth, Purakaunui Bay
Beach breaks.
Off. N to W.
Tides vary.
Loc. SE of Owaka off State Highway 92.

### 288 Long Point
Good left point break.
Off. NE.
Best at low tide.
Loc. South of Owaka off State Highway 92..

### 289 Papatowai
River mouth — beach break.
Off. NW to SW.
Best at high tide.
Loc. off State Highway 92.
Camping ground.

**PLEASE NOTE:**

A largely unexplored area, the Catlins region is well worth a look. Long Point in particular is one of the better lefthanders in the South Island and can hold a sizeable swell. There is also a reef with potential between Papatowai and Tautuku, but access is difficult.

# INVERCARGILL — MAP U

### 290 Colac Bay
Beach break.
Off. NW.
All tides on a medium to large swell.

### 291 Nicks Point
Right point break.
Off. NW to SW.
Best at half to low tide on a large W to SW swell.
Loc. South of Colac.

### 292 Spot X
Right reef break.
Off. NE to NW.
Best at half to low tide on a small to medium swell.
Access through farm (summer only) — be nice to the farmer!
Loc. SW of Colac.

### 293 Beatons
Left point break.
Off. SE to NE.
Best at half to low tide on a small to medium swell.
Access through farm — be nice to the farmer!
Loc. South of Orepuki.

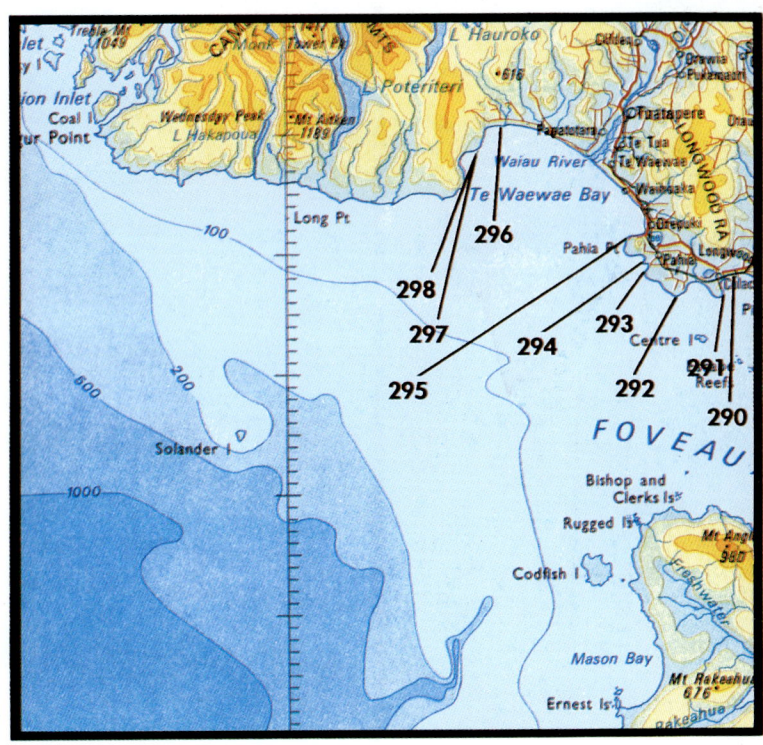

### 294 Porridge
Left point break.
Off. SE to NE.
High tide, only on large swell.
Access through farm (summer only) —
be nice to the farmer!
Loc. South of Orepuki.

### 295 Frentzes
Left point break.
Off. S to E.
Best at half to low tide on a large
westerley swell.
Loc. SW of Orepuki.

### 296 Bluecliffs
Right point break.
Off. NE to NW.
Best at high tide on a large swell.
Access on beach road only —
sometimes hazardous.
Loc. NW of Orepuki.

### 297 2nd Break
Right point break.
Off. NW to W.
Anytide on a large SW to S swell.
Access on beach road only —sometimes
hazardous.
Loc. NW of Orepuki.

### 298 3rd Break
Right point break.
Off. NW to W.
Best at low tide on a large SW to S
swell.
Access on beach road — sometimes
hazardous.
Loc. NW of Orepuki.

**PLEASE NOTE:**

As can be expected this area receives
some heavy swells and luckily has a few
breaks that can handle the considerable
energy of the southern ocean. The
locals surf all year round due to the
warm Trans-Tasman current flowing
through Foveaux Strait. Camping
grounds are at Tuatapere, Colac Bay
and Riverton. Garages are at Riverton,
Orepuki and Tuatapere.

## STEWART ISLAND

Definitely the last frontier of New
Zealand surfing breaks. However there
is surf there but you'll need a boat as
there are no roads and a local as a
guide as it is not a safe place for
beginners. The South East coast would
have the most potential.

# THE WEST COAST — MAP V

### 299 Blaketown
Right bar break.
Off. NE to E.
Best at low tide.
Loc. at South Greymouth Breakwater.
Acc. and garage at Greymouth.

### 300 Cobden
Left bar break.
Off. NE to S.
Tides vary with sandbars.
Loc. at North Greymouth Breakwater.
Acc. and garage at Greymouth.

### 301 Rapahoe
Beach break.
Off. S to E.
Tide varies with sandbars.
Loc. 12 kms North of Greymouth on
State Highway 6.

### 302 Nine Mile
Left point break.
Off. E.
Best middle to low tide.
Loc. North side of Nine Mile Bluff.
Acc. and garage at Greymouth.

### 303 Punakaiki
Two beach breaks.
Off. NE to E.
Best at low tide on a small swell.
Loc. between Greymouth and
Westport.
Acc. and garage at Punakaiki.

### 304 Fox River
Left river bar break.
Off. S to E.
Tide varies with sandbars.
Loc. at Fox River mouth on State

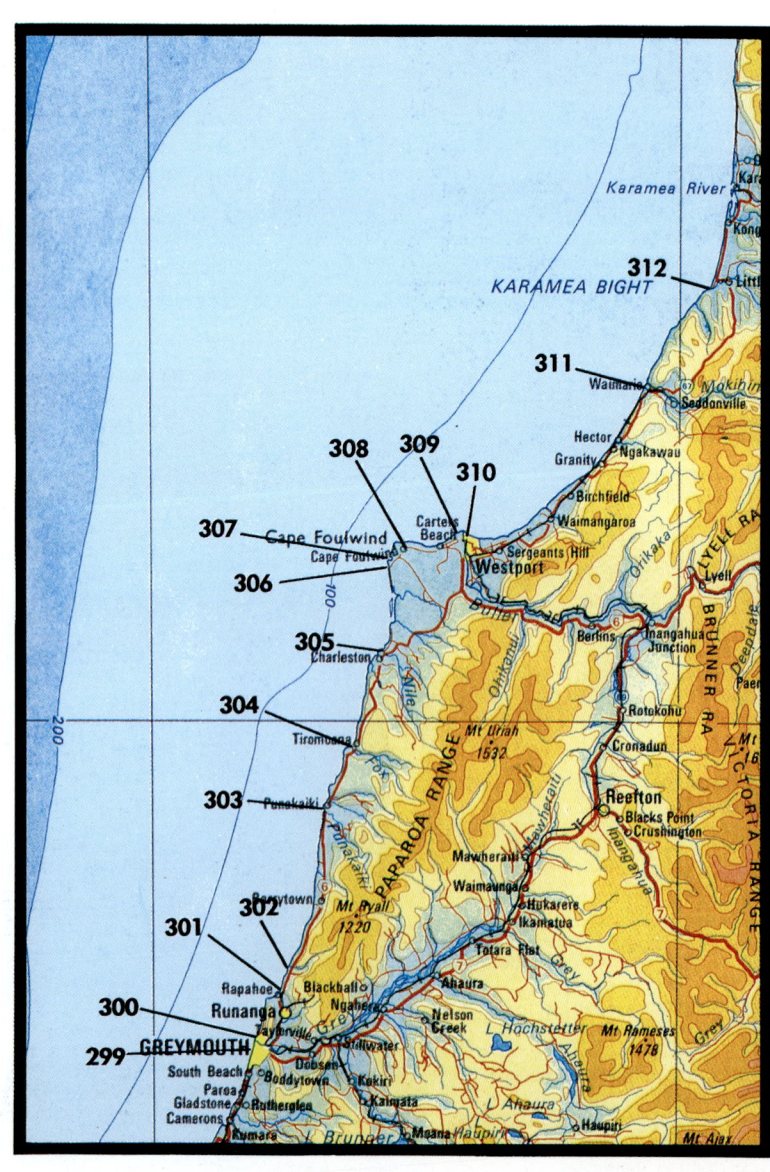

Highway 6.
Acc. and garage at Punakaiki.

## 305 Charleston
Beach and river bar break.
Off. S to E.
Tide varies with sandbars.
Loc. at Charleston on State Highway 6.
Acc. and garage at Charleston.

## 306 Nine Mile Beach
Good beach break.
Off. NE to E.
Best at high tide.
Loc. SW of Westport, and just over the hill from Tauranga Bay.
Acc. and garage at Westport.

## 307 Tauranga Bay
Left point to beach break.
Off. S to E.
Tide varies with sandbars.
Loc. SW of Westport.
Acc. and garage at Westport.

## 308 Larsen Street
Beach break.
Off. S to E.
Tide varies with sandbars.
Loc. opposite Cement Works at Westport.
Acc. and garage at Westport.

## 309 Shingles
Beach break.
Off. S to E.
Best tide varies.
Loc. 1 km inside the Buller River Breakwater.
Acc. and garage at Westport.

## 310 Westport Breakwater
Beach break.
Off. S to E.
Tide varies — strong northerly drift.
Loc. at Westport.
Acc. and garage at Westport.

# NORTH WEST COAST — MAP W

## 311 Waimarie
River bar break.
Off. E.
Best tide varies.
Loc. 60 kms North of Westport.
Acc. and garage at Waimarie.

## 312 Little Wanganui
Good river bar break.
Off. S to E.
Best tide varies.
Loc. 100 kms North of Westport.
Acc. and garage at Little Wanganui.

## 313 Wairaiki Beach
Beach break, exposed.
Off. E.
Good on all tides.

Loc. approx. 150 kms West of Nelson.
Poor access through a farm.
Acc. and garage at Collingwood.

## 314 Fergusons Beach
Beach break, exposed.
Off. E.
Good on all tides.
Loc. 148 kms West of Nelson. Pool access through a farm.
Acc. and garage at Collingwood.

## 315 Farewell Spit
Left beach break, exposed.
Off. E.
Good on incoming tide only (beware of rips).
Loc. North of Puponga.
Acc. and garage at Collingwood.

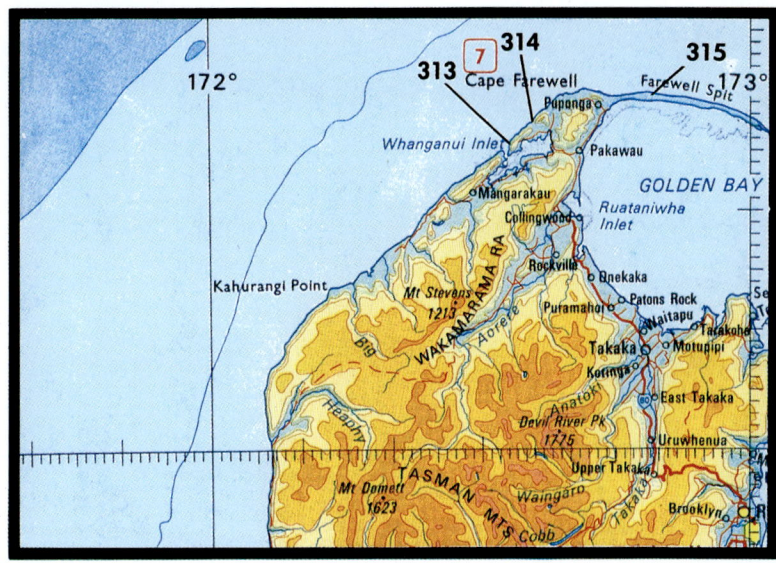

*Cobden Breakwater, Greymouth*

## PLEASE NOTE:
The West Coast of the South Island is unusual from a surfing viewpoint, as one often has to wait for the swell to drop sufficiently to make surfing possible. This beautiful and dramatic coastline unfortunately does not have too many big wave spots especially from Greymouth northwards. Very little is known about the South West coast apart from rumour and conjecture, but there are however, a few accessible spots from Harihari south, surf knowledge and a good map will help you to discover them.

Surfer Nuku Nash

# BOOK CATALOGUE—VIKING SEVENSEAS LTD

## P.O. BOX 152 or 23B IHAKARA STREET, PARAPARAUMU. TEL. AND FAX: (04) 297-1990.

### RETAIL PRICE LIST (G.S.T. INCLUSIVE)

**NEW RELEASES** (In boxes)

### NEW ZEALAND POCKET GUIDES (Each $6.25)

CAKE DECORATING GUIDE — Book One (S049)
..........................Dorothy Beatty

FLORA AND FAUNA OF NEW ZEALAND (S032)
..........................Glen Pownall

JADE TREASURES OF THE MAORI (S090) .....Murdoch Riley

KIWI AND MOA — Two Unique Birds (S071) .....Murdoch Riley

KIWI COOKBOOK — N.Z. Recipes (S016).......Alan Armstrong

KNOW YOUR MAORI CARVING (S069) .............Glen Pownall

KNOW YOUR NEW ZEALAND BIRDS (S068) ...Murdoch Riley

MAORI CUSTOMS AND CRAFTS (S009) ........Alan Armstrong

MAORI LEGENDS — Maui & Others (S017) ..Alistair Campbell

MAORI SONGBOOK — Seventy Songs (S014)
..........................Sam Freedman

MAORI VEGETABLE COOKING (S093) ............Murdoch Riley

NEW ZEALAND TREES AND FERNS (S073) ....Murdoch Riley

NEW ZEALAND WAYS WITH FLOWERS (S075)
..........................Eileen Dobson

NEW ZEALAND WILDLIFE (S070).....................Murdoch Riley

SAY IT IN MAORI — Phrasebook (S010) .........Alan Armstrong

SHRUBS AND SMALL TREES (S076) ...............Murdoch Riley

SUCCESSFUL CAKE DECORATING, BK.2 (S074)
..........................Dorothy Beatty

WEKA WON'T LEARN — For Children (S047) ....Maxine Schur

### NEW ZEALAND BOOKS

| | | |
|---|---|---|
| CAMERA ON ROTORUA (B092)..................Shari & Don Cole | | 4.00 |
| GAMES AND DANCES OF THE MAORI PEOPLE: Detailed instructional manual (B088) .................Alan Armstrong | | 17.95 |
| HINEMOA AND TUTANEKAI (B045) .............Harold Callender | | 2.20 |
| KNOW YOUR SOUTH ISLAND PLACES (B096) Murdoch Riley | | 15.95 |
| MAORI GAMES — English language (B039) .......Colin Deed | | 6.25 |
| MAORI GAMES — Maori language (B040) ............Colin Deed | | 6.25 |
| MAORI HEALING AND HERBAL – Hb. (B095) Murdoch Riley | | 79.95 |
| MAORI SAYINGS AND PROVERBS (B094) ......Murdoch Riley | | 9.95 |
| MOANA — Novel of old N. Z. days (B030)...........Barry Mitcalfe | | 6.25 |
| MUSIC OF THE MAORI: Origins (B034) .............Dr. T. Barrow | | 9.95 |
| NEATH THE MANTLE OF RANGI (B036) ...........Brian Enting | | 17.95 |
| NEUSEELANDS MAORI ABC (S098) .............Murdoch Riley | | 7.95 |
| NEW ZEALAND TREES & FERNS — Hb. (B072) Murdoch Riley | | 9.95 |
| UNIQUE NEW ZEALAND: Its Story (B003) .........Glen Pownall | | 9.95 |
| WITCH AT THE WELLINGTON LIBRARY (B066) Maxine Schur | | 4.00 |

### SOUVENIR COMPACT DISCS

TWENTY FIVE SOLID GOLD MAORI SONGS Top Groups
377CD

MAORI LOVE SONGS Wiki/St. Josephs
409CD

BIRDS OF NEW ZEALAND — & 12 p. booklet Land & sea birds
445CD

KIA ORA — HELLO! GOOD HEALTH! 34 songs Turakina Girls
486CD

POKAREKARE: A love song & 30 others NZ Maori Chorale
487CD

### CASSETTE/POCKET GUIDE COMBINATIONS (Each $17.50)

BIRDS OF NEW ZEALAND — 18 bird calls and colour booklet
of 64 pages Land & sea birds VPS445CB..................

HAERE MAI! — 20 music tracks & 30 page booklet on action
songs, haka etc. Top groups VPS475C ................

HERITAGE OF MAORI SONGS — Words & music for
28 songs, cassette/booklet Various groups SPR 40C...............

### SOUVENIR CASSETTES (Each $15.50)

Denotes best sellers **

MAORI SONGS OF ENCHANTMENT St. Josephs Girls
VPS 52C .................

POKAREKARE ** St. Josephs Girls VPS162C .................

TRADITIONAL MUSIC OF THE MAORI Nose flute & songs
VPS243C .................

TWENTY SOLID GOLD MAORI SONGS ** Famous Maori
groups VPS377C .................

NOW IS THE HOUR Ngararanui Cultural VPS378C ...............

POKAREKARE N.Z. Maori Chorale VPS388C.................

TWENTY GOLDEN MAORI SONGS Famous Maori groups
VPS406C .................

MAORI LOVE SONGS ** with Wiki Baker St. Josephs Girls
VPS409C .................

SONGS OF NEW ZEALAND ** N.Z. Maori Chorale VPS425C .

NEW ZEALAND SINGS N.Z. Maori Chorale VPS431C.............

JOY OF MAORI SONG Turakina Girls VPS446C .................

HAERE MAI! WELCOME! Hokowhitu-Atu Party VPS477C .......

MAORI MEMORIES: GOLDEN 50'S MOMENTS Te Aute,
Waipatu . . . VPS482C .................

GOLD AWARD MAORI SONGS N.Z. Maori Chorale 1001C.....

GOLD AWARD MAORI SONGS, VOL. 2
Maori Theatre Trust 1002C .................

FAMOUS MAORI SONGS Rangatira Maori C5001.................

A PROGRAMME OF MAORI SONGS ** Maori Theatre Trust
C5063 .................

### POLYNESIAN SHEET MUSIC AND WORDS (Each $7.95)

POLYNESIAN MUSIC: 63 songs, 84 p. (A052) .................

SOLID GOLD MAORI SONGS: Top 12 (A053) .................

SONGS OF THE SOUTH SEAS (A051) .................

### PICTORIAL BOOKLETS (Each $1.95)

AUSTRALIA IN COLOUR (C058) .................

BEAUTIFUL NEW ZEALAND (C000).................

COLOURFUL NEW ZEALAND (C001) .................

COLOUR COUNTRY (C044).................

COLOUR PAGEANT (C043) .................

COLOUR PANORAMA (C041).................

COLOUR SPECTACLE (C042) .................

LOVE LEGENDS OF THE MAORI (C056).................

ROTORUA — SIGHTS (C057).................